Management Workstations
for Greater Productivity

Other McGraw-Hill Books by the Author

Designing and Implementing Local Area Networks (1984)

Interactive Message Services (1984)

Management Workstations for Greater Productivity

by Dimitris N. Chorafas

McGraw-Hill Book Company

New York   St. Louis   San Francisco   Auckland
Bogotá   Hamburg   Johannesburg   London   Madrid
Mexico   Montreal   New Delhi   Panama   Paris
São Paulo   Singapore   Sydney   Tokyo   Toronto

Photographs reproduced on the part title pages are provided cour-
tesy of IBM, Olivetti, and DEC and are reprinted with permission.

Library of Congress Cataloging in Publication Data
Chorafas, Dimitris N.
  Management workstations for greater productivity.

  Includes index.
  1. Management—Data processing. 2. Office practice—
Automation. 3. Microcomputers. I. Title.
HD30.2.C48 1986   658'.054   85–159
ISBN 0–07–010859–5

ISBN 0-07-010859-5

The editors for this book were Martha Jewett and Galen H. Fleck;
the designer was Mark E. Safran; and the production supervisor
was Thomas Kowalczyk. It was set in Baskerville by Kingsport Press.

Printed and bound by R. R. Donnelley & Sons, Inc.

To
Harold D. Koontz, Louis Sorel and
Neil Jacoby, my professors
from whom I learned
the art of management

Contents

Preface

Industries contending with advances in technology must sharpen the *mental productivity* of their managers in order to grow and survive. This calls for a thorough, well-coordinated strategy that is both market-oriented and technology-based.

Computers and communications are the agents and the vehicles of change. We know from experience that the more diverse technological components are the greater the information exchange that has to take place to master them. At premium is the ability to identify a problem and then deploy the organizational resources needed to handle it. That is the reason for the emphasis on mental productivity.

When we talk about the new computers and communications technologies, our first and foremost concern should be for the end user. That is the baseline with personal computers (PCs), local area networks (LANs), and fourth-generation languages (4GLs). Goals and applications drive the development of a system. Given the dual aspect of a competitive corporate strategy and of technological achievements, the aim of this book is to demonstrate how computers and communications can be used effectively to boost information exchanges and thereby broaden the horizons of the human mind.

This book is addressed to the busy manager who both wants and needs to learn what technology can offer in a broad area affecting his or her work: intelligent workstations (WSs), integrated software (Isoft), decision support systems (DSSs), electronic mail (Email), and private branch exchanges (PBXs). In a comprehensive way, it demonstrates and documents how and why technology serves a purpose in office automation: applying computer power to problems that presently require costly and time-consuming paperwork.

Office work involves six phases: the creation of a document, its physical presence, its distribution within the firm, its storage, its retrieval, and its distribution external to the firm. These phases are often interlaced. Their proper identification calls for a reorganization of internal systems and procedures and for review of external communications. That is what the reader obtains in 16 chapters written in an easy and comprehensible manner. By means of practical examples, he or she is guided through the procedural steps taken by companies which currently work on office automation and interactive communications projects. The reader is presented with the results those companies have achieved, the cost-effectiveness of the outcome, and the importance of user-friendly approaches when we talk of an implementation at the workplace.

In Part 1 we will look at the needs of management: What is the reason for intelligent workstations? The opening chapter has to do with information workers and information tools. The following chapter explains why the product we wish to get from high technology is *information faster, more accurately, and more efficiently*—it is neither software nor hardware details. Better information is obtained through machines able to assist the human mind (Chapter 3). That assistance is given in an office environment. But there are facts and fiction about office automation, as the following chapter suggests.

In Chapter 5, the discussion centers on productivity goals. There is *clerical* (or physical) and *mental productivity*. Which is the more important? If the steam engine was the key machine of the industrial age, the clock is the hub of post-industrial society. Orderly punctual life, which first occurred in monasteries, is not native to mankind—though by now the West has been so regimented by the clock that living by it has become second nature. "Time," we say, is "money."

The computer is the information extension of the clock. It is a product of technology, and technology can be a friend or a foe depending on our attitude. The computer is not the cold neighbor that the "giant brain" imagery once suggested. *It is the lens of the mind's eye.*

The objective of Part 2 is to see how high technology affects management practice. Is management changing the way it used to handle information systems (Chapter 6)? One sure change has come about through the substitution of computer-based workstations for paper and dumb terminals, as we will see in Chapter 7. But management, the next chapter explains, has its own viewpoints. They are not necessarily those of the computer experts.

Decision support systems are discussed in Chapter 9, and in Chapter 10 suggestions are made on where expert systems may be useful. Expert systems are the pivot point around which the fifth computer generation will be built by the mid-1990s.

The aim of Part 3 is to give the reader some down-to-earth practical examples on how to use intelligent workstations. First and foremost we must adapt our images and concepts to the opportunities offered by the new technology (Chapter 11). Then we must use the new tools to our advantage. This cannot be done by preaching the Gospel. It takes training and practice, and training in the usage of high technology should be increasingly oriented toward the management level (Chapter 12). That's where we can expect the best results.

Chapter 13 focuses on integrated software and fourth-generation languages. For the end user, the most friendly way to program is by visual thinking (Chapter 14). The following chapter explains why there is a significant drive toward graphics applications.

Chapter 16 is addressed to the manager from a different viewpoint: that of policies which are necessary, services that must be provided, and the all-important financial evaluation. *The acid test of any system is: Does it pay?*

User-friendly interactive message systems are the link to the development of the effective decision support capabilities. They offer *the critical characteristics management needs for reasons of mental productivity:* immediate response, graphics and color presentation, directional sense, and security and protection. They are *ideal for flexible exception reporting,* giving management the information it needs when it needs it.

* * *

May I close this introduction by expressing my thanks to everybody who contributed to this book: my colleagues for their advice, the organizations I visited in my research for their insight, and Eva-Maria Binder for the drawings and the typing of the manuscript.

Valmer and Vitznau DIMITRIS N. CHORAFAS

PART 1

Why Do We Need
Intelligent Workstations?

CHAPTER 1

Information Workers and Information Tools

A proverb is a short sentence based on long experience.

CERVANTES

According to the Stanford Research Institute, in the United States alone there are 37 million white-collar workers who are prime candidates to be users of intelligent workstations. Their numbers are growing at the rate of 2 percent per year. The need to stop this personnel explosion is evident to everybody—and so are the challenges. They can be met with a distributed information system.

A *workstation* (WS) is the centerpiece of the distributed information system. It makes feasible personal computing, the beneficiary of which is the actual user of the system as an individual.

Typically personal-computer-based as it is, a workstation provides its services through software. The software has now become a readily available commodity, and fourth-generation languages (4GL) tremendously ease the problem of instructing the machine.*

The biggest issue of all, the one that effects all the others, is the need to get senior management directly and actively involved in a strat-

---

* For a résumé of computer terminology, see the Technical Notes section, which closes the chapter. Similar sections close many other chapters, and abbreviations are listed in the Appendix.

3

egy of improving office management. There are simply too many things that cannot be done without such active participation.

Furthermore, there is a need for unification in the line of command. In the past, different people were responsible for word processing, data processing, and communications. Now one executive should have authority over all those activities.

Also in the past, computers and communications products and services were supplied by a wide variety of vendors. To take care of word processing, the office manager purchased typewriters, copiers, dictaphones, and file cabinets. To take care of data processing, the head of accounting bought computers. A telephone executive looked after the telephones, private branch exchange, and relations with the public utility.

At least as far as the sources of supply are concerned, the move is now toward unification and its pace will accelerate over the coming years. National and international accords tend to create entities which can look after personal computers (PCs) and mainframes, local area networks and private branch exchanges (PBXs), word, data, and image processors, electronic mail, and voice mail, as well as a wide range of other products.

Because of the great diversity of offerings, and also because we are at the cutting edge of technology, establishing a successful information system depends on having

- A clear plan
- Top-management support
- Administrative consolidation

Without the system to which these things are prerequisites, the office will have an increasingly negative effect on the bottom line. With it, the office will be positioned to make its contribution to the success of the enterprise.

Information Policies

Information system planning must be anchored in business strategy. The approach to operations should not just guide information system policies but determine them. Information policies must support the overall operation: staffing, systems requirements, and communications procedures. The business plan must set up the milestones on the path toward reaching the company's overall goals.

To do its job successfully, the *office automation (OA) planning team* should include senior executives from every functional area of the busi-

4

ness, and it must have the direct support and involvement of the chief executive officer. A top level steering committee should act as the *OA review council,* and it should include key technologies such as:

- Software
- Personal computers
- Word processing (WP)
- Communications
- Databases
- Systems engineering
- Systems integration

It would, however, be wrong to assume that because we set up a task force, there will be results. A task force has to be carefully managed and steered in order to produce any tangible outcome of its efforts. Furthermore, to implement the task force principle, management should provide some guidelines. Both the logical and the physical kind are advisable.

Mobil Oil has given us an example of what it takes to remain competitive even if a company starts with a good data processing (DP) system. Its chief executive, Mr. Gardner, gave all his top people personal computers to help them increase their productivity. With training, almost every Mobil Oil executive came to

- Love the PC
- Use it to increase personal productivity
- Use it to improve the quality of work

A similar training program took place at United Technologies, where 1000 senior managers underwent a 3-day training course on the PC and its software. Wisely, top management made a present of a PC to every person who completed the course.

These are only two of the increasing number of managements that are taking the opportunity to increase productivity and improve the quality of service. For many organizations, the objective over time is to have a *professional workstation* network. Financial institutions and industrial companies with clear information policies want this aggregate of WSs to be able to communicate directly with minicomputers and mainframes. Their plans focus on the top level rather than on the clerical level.

Benefits can be much more impressive at the top level, which accounts for the direction being taken by so many major organizations.

5

TABLE 1

Users	1984, %	1990, %
Presidents	3	20
Vice presidents	10	40
Managers	20	75

As you will see in Table 1, the forecast is that WS users at the president level will increase nearly 700 percent by 1990, whereas for middle management the projected increase stands at 375 percent.

Some firms have already installed WS, and local area networks (LANs) at the top-management level. An example is Bangor Punta. Others provide intensive hands-on experience. Among banks, the Mellon Bank has established a computer literacy program. The Bank of Boston, in a major step toward realizing the goal of having microcomputer communications capabilities, negotiated with several vendors for the development and implementation of microcomputer-to-mainframe linkages. It also aims to assure data integrity and security throughout all the layers of computer systems being put into operation at the bank.

In many organizations, the use of electronic mail (Email) is gathering momentum, and Email is followed by computer conferencing and calendaring services. In a way, these three areas of application have in common the drive to relieve managers of the load placed upon them by various types of meetings. As a research project demonstrated, only 52 percent of management meetings are scheduled—an impressive 48 percent are nonscheduled. Participants found that:

- Only 19 percent of scheduled meetings are conducted with agendas.
- 35 percent of all meetings are too long.
- 34 percent of meetings are nonproductive.

Time savings are easily translated into financial savings. Managers at all levels represent 21 percent of the 51 million white-collar population in the United States, but their salaries represent 27 percent of the $15 billion spent weekly on payrolls (Table 2). The 51 million white-collar workers generate 91 billion documents per year. In turn, the documents are reproduced in 149 billion copies with an average of 2.8 pages each. Together the copies account for 23 billion pieces of mail, about 25 percent of the total.

The above-mentioned documents, copies, and pieces of mail constitute entities which must be filed and eventually retrieved; and together they represent 482 billion pages per year. If written on 8.5- by 11-inch

TABLE 2   U.S. white-collar workers: 51 million persons with $15 billion weekly payroll

	Percent of population	Percent of payroll
Managers	21	27
Professionals	31	36
Salespeople	12	12
Secretaries, clerks	36	25
	100	100

With the number of new documents growing at the rate of 20 to 22 percent per year, the total volume of information stored doubles every 4 years. Every working day, U.S. businesses generate an estimated:
- 600 million pages of printed computer output
- 76 million letters

(21.6- by 28-centimeter) paper, at 80 grams per square meter, they amount to 2.41 million tons (2.66 metric tons) of paper per year.

The PCs present us with an opportunity to cut these statistics down to size provided the PCs are used properly and implementation is the object of a careful study:

- They are relatively inexpensive.
- They can be employed for good purposes.
- They help improve the productivity of managers.

Also, they offer their users valuable assistance in understanding the information they get. The computer has lessened the lag between the development of a service and its commercialization. Managers and professionals see the PC-based workstation as a combination of word processing, personal computing, spreadsheet-based experimentation and analysis communications, and graphics. Individualized decision support systems are foremost in their thinking.

The True Data Processor

After more than three decades of computer experience, we are finally finding the true data processor. It is the *intelligent workstation* with a capacity to move text, data, and graphics around and with linkage to a mainframe for extended databasing capabilities. Acting as big communications switches, the mainframes are handling text and data for people to work with.

In the process of putting an intelligent WS on every desk, the PC has come to occupy a unique position. Through the power of its microprocessor and with a wealth of easy-to-use business software, it provides solutions for today's manager while changing the way business is perceived and conducted.

Anything we can put in a PC, we can put in it as a file. In terms of implementation potential, its databasing and data communication capability (DB/DC) exceeds its data processing capability. Because of the price at which it is offered, PC represents the single most important input/output (I/O) technology for the middle to late 1980s.

PC functionality in a *terminal* sense is foremost in importance. In retrospect, during two decades of evolution, terminals have progressed from being dumb to being smart and finally to being intelligent. But intelligent terminals have different degrees of ability to handle dumb connections, local storage of downloading with only error control, structuring and formatting downloaded data, local work on data local formatting prior to sending upline, microfiles, microfiles with database management system (DBMS) capability; use of DBMS as a programming language with run time, a variety of communications protocols, and simultaneous processing and communications with one or more mainframes.

Historically, the earliest approach—the only one possible—was to put dumb terminals to work by using shared logic. This worked well for automating some secretarial work, but it did not serve the needs of managers. With nonintelligent terminals access to corporate data files proved too slow, even at 9.6 kBPS (kilo, or thousand, bits per second).

The next solution involved a network of minicomputers which supported multiple terminals. However, although each minicomputer could support several users, the requirements of networking used up half of each computer's power. Therefore, the minicomputer proved to be an inefficient solution which soon reached its limits.

The third solution was to give PCs to everyone. That led to the discovery that data had to be shared; we needed networks so that we could gain access to information. The realization led to the fourth approach: PCs and LANs with long-haul connections.

PCs can operate in either the stand-alone or the remote mode; they can provide services ranging from work processing and spreadsheets to electronic mail, calendaring, and graphics. But in the long run their implementation will be successful only if there is proper support for effective communications.

From a superficial view, manufacturers appear to offer unique products. Prices range from $1000 to $3000 for simple PCs, from $3000 to $6000 for units supporting hard disk and data communications interfaces, and from $8000 to $12,000 for supermicros. The multitasking, multiuser features of the latter systems are achieved by having an appropriate operating system, such as Unix, and by having a more powerful microprocessor that divides its time among several different tasks.

In the lower-cost category, some machines utilize both 8 and 16 bits per word (BPW) processors. In mid-range products, auxiliary processors handle input/output (I/O) functions while the main microprocessor does the calculations. Through successive models, the mid-range PCs have been moving from the 8 BPW of 1980 and 1981 toward 16 BPW in 1983 and 1984, with 32 BPW promising to be the fastest-growing segment in 1986 and 1987. At the same time, there is a significant movement away from nonintelligent terminals toward PC-based intelligent workstations (Figure 1).

Most important, this growth in PC capacity and potential has been compensated by technological advances so that price has remained practically stable. The typical $5000 workstation in early 1985 represented:

Microprocessor	16 BPW
Power	0.2 to 0.3 million instructions per second
Central memory (CM)	128 to 256 Kbytes (K = 1024)
Auxiliary memory	10 to 20 Mbytes (M = mega or million)
Screen	0.25 to 0.35 Mpixels

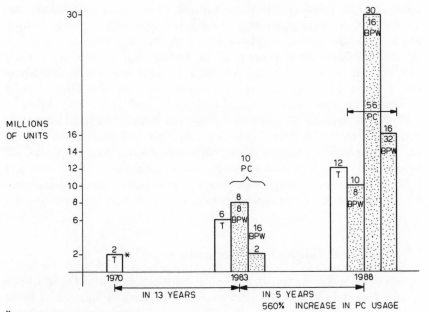

*T = NONINTELLIGENT TERMINALS

FIGURE 1. Projected evolution in demand for 32-BPW (bits per word) PCs.

In the 1987 to 1988 timeframe, the same money can be expected to buy:

Microprocessor	32 BPW
Power	1 MIPS
Central memory	1 Mbyte
Auxiliary memory	60 Mbytes
Screen	1 Mpixels

In 1983 and 1984 that was equivalent to an engineering workstation for computer-aided design and manufacturing (CAD/CAM) applications often costing $25,000. In about 1986 to 1987 the $25,000 engine will be a symbolic machine with:

- Central memory, 6 Mbytes
- Auxiliary memory, 200 Mbytes
- Voice I/O
- User-generated computing

allowing fast development of algorithms and heuristics. By the end of this decade the programming concepts of the preceding three decades will be alien to this machine. You will tell the machine the results you want, and the relational database will ask the necessary questions and do the job. An expert systems orientation, originally a research tool, will become the common approach to everyday problem solving.

Behind these developments is the 1-Mbit chip announced in early 1984 by Japanese manufacturers. Now in sight are 50- to 500-Kbyte components on a chip that will cost only a few dollars. There will be continued improvements in speed and power and high-density storage: 100 million pages at 30 Kbytes per page for 2 cents per page is roughly equivalent to 0.000000085 cent per bit. This will profoundly change the way we look at computers and communications. Minicomputers will be obsolete and the mainframes also for anything other than acting as DB/DC machines. Table 3 identifies trends in pricing and the expected 1-year improvement per type of product.

Physical and Logical Workstations

In business and industry, the simplest application of the PC has been financial modeling through spreadsheets. The data should not be input manually. It should come online from the database of a mainframe

TABLE 3   Pricing trends in instruction execution
at 1 MIPS

Computer type	Mid-1983 $ × 1000	1-year improvement, %
Mainframes	300	20
Minis	100	20
Micros*	30	30

Storage capability per megabyte		
Mainframes	30	20
Minis	150	15
Micros*	220	30

* With 1984's micros, 0.3 MIPS cost about $3000; but in 1985 to 1987,
1.0 MIPS will cost the same amount.

NOTE: The data flow rates are as follows:

Computer type	No. of simult. disk I/O	Peak megabytes per second
Mainframe	4 to 32	4 to 160
Mini (now crashed)	1 to 2	1 to 8
Micro	1	0.2 to 1

or mini—hence through shared storage. This can be achieved by using
the PC:

- As an emulation of a nonintelligent terminal
- As a window run on an intelligent WS looking into the mainframe.

In the preceding section, I spoke of the different degrees of intelligent PC–to–mainframe connection. Either of the above two approaches can write a bottom line. Higher-up facilities call for formatting and editing capabilities realized in a programmable coordinated manner based on the PC. A still higher level of sophistication is to use the PC to really offload DP and DB from the mainframe. Divesting the mainframe of many of its classical applications can result in both dollar savings and better performance.

Yet it cannot be repeated too often that imaginative implementation will never happen all by itself. We must thoroughly assess both the current and the possible applications in this enormous field and devise strategies for making them work.

Professional and managerial computing requires the combining of readily affordable PCs with professional quality software. This integration is the key to satisfying the current requirements and eventually using expert systems not only to suggest solutions but also to document and justify the answers they give.

This brings us to the definition, in both the physical and the logical sense, of the *workstation* on which personal computing is done. The physical workstation is a visual display unit

- Containing a single-board computer dedicated to the application required by the user
- Including disk storage
- Incorporating communications devices and other I/O media

The logical workstation is:

- The address of all input
- Local storage (microfiles)
- Personal computing routines
- Output operations

Together the logical and physical characteristics define the functions of the workstation. Database languages, spreadsheets, and packages that produce financial planning and color graphics have put WS functions in an entirely new light. The workstation has become much more than at-hand electronics, and it has given data processing a totally new dimension.

Executives often get where they are because of their analytical abilities, but they rarely make full use of those abilities on the job because they lack the right tools. This is the number 1 issue when we talk of the WS: analytical ability is well supported by personal computing. The next important issue is communications, and the third is databasing. Each imposes different demands on

1. *Information exchange*
2. *Response time*
3. *Internal processing*

These are the three key variables of interest at the professional workstation.

It will not be an easy task to rid ourselves of the bad practices of 30 years, yet somehow we must now learn:

- *To stop programming the devices to do only what we think they are capable of doing, like number crunching and producing reams of printout*
- *To start programming the devices for the unique applications we should expect of them*

Applications programs should be retained on hard disk and loaded to the central memory when called up by the user. They should then execute under a single operating system (OS) in the workstation. The concept of concurrent operation permits simultaneous input, storage, processing, and output.

Careful attention should be given to two key points on which some users fail to focus when they initiate the WS experience. That is most unfortunate, because they are fundamental:

> First, there is no room for two terminals on the desk. One must do all the work.

For instance, the use of PC and WP software makes the employment of independent word processors unwise. The same thing is true of terminals for electronic mail and a host of other applications.

The classical approach to word processing has been dumb terminals. That is very expensive, and it can be excused only when the objective is just to automate the secretarial work—which is in itself a very near-sighted approach. On the contrary, every WS—whatever its *current* assignment—should have capabilities which make it easily interfaceable. We should rely on software to capitalize on the hardware.

Quite similarly, we should capitalize on the fact that computer products are convergent. *We must look on the PC as an integral part of the mainframe resources.* The need for continual communication between PC and mainframes derives from this simple premise.

In the early days of telephony, rich people had two or three phones, one for each telephone company in town. It was the only way to communicate with other people who had a telephone service. A similar situation exists today, this time with computer terminals. We must, however, realize that *integrating these machines is our challenge.* A system plan should include both the sources and the destinations of information. A network of equipment that intercommunicates easily will smooth out the flow of information, whether it be text, data, voice, images, or charts. If we do the work right, we will see vast improvement in the quality of the information we provide and get.

> Second, there is significant room for improvement in system response time—the time the user waits. The end user should not be obliged to wait for the information he or she asks for.

System response time is measured from the point at which the user signals the system that there is work to be done to the point at which the system begins to present the results asked for. This delay time should be kept to 1 or 2 seconds at most. Within a given operating environment, a basic system response time should be computed to identify the prevailing operating characteristics. The definition should include:

1. Job(s) being treated
2. Input needs, including formatting and assistance with errors
3. File access in relation to the physical media used and the logical supports
4. Logical capabilities including those related to database management systems (DBMS)

Other critical characteristics are time for output, type of access (remote versus local), chosen communications protocols, and front-end machine capabilities.

The Universal Workstation

By integrating the different terminal functions—and therefore distinct physical terminals—on the same PC, we can improve system response time. But the most impressive way to decrease response time delays is to place dedicated personal computer power and databasing capabilities at the user's site. The goal should be *a universal workstation optimized by function.* The same WS should be installed for and used by managers, professionals, and supporting staff. Software accounts for user differences. The secretary needs word processing capabilities; the broker wants market data; the manager requires planning tools. These different requirements do not mean that terminals must be different.

Actually, the people working in an organization have many functions in common. Thus all of the functions on the secretary's terminal, with the exception of word processing, will be on the broker's. The brokers do not need word processing. But they do require:

- Query capabilities
- Electronic mail
- Electronic filing
- Calendar management
- Decision support
- Expert systems

Again—and it cannot be said too often—the system should be designed to increase productivity within the perspectives of a strategic plan. Said the senior executive of a brokerage firm: "We have reached a point where there is less of a payback in geographic expansion than in diversifying the products that the brokers use, improving their productivity on an individual basis."

In this and similar cases the goal is to use automation at the office level to enable the professionals to produce more. That means supporting them with computers and communications services. Since the workstations will be tied into the public telephone network, they can be used to send and receive messages. They can access public databases such as Dow Jones, Reuters, Telerate, Autex, UPI, and Press Release News Wire. They can store information on microfiles, and they can do personal computing.

A whole infrastructure must be created to support this system in an able manner. For instance, calendar management software may be needed to coordinate meetings and save executive time. Most important, a system administrator is necessary to decide who can set and change calendars. Similar observations apply to running a realtime spreadsheet for budgetary control, supporting an interdepartmental *project management* package, and featuring voice datatypes leading toward *voice editing* and *voice mail.*

For an electronic mail (Email) connection, a shell must be created so the WP/Email link is transparent to the secretary and can be called up by a simple command. But still more important is to provide an encryption capability through either an algorithmic solution or software and/or hardware (SW/HW) approaches provided by the vendor. *Encryption capability* means passwords, authorization, and authentication. It also means the document will be garbled and impossible to read without the right password. These are vital issues to be settled before—not after—instituting the new computers and communications aggregate.

Encryption capabilities are particularly important in long-haul communications between, for instance, the resources in the central computer and those in the branches, sales offices, and factories or installed at customer organizations (CO). As Figure 2 outlines, the environment is unique, and it should be treated as such whether we talk of software or hardware implementation affecting the whole system.

More precisely, although hardware should be universal, the software should vary not by form but by function. Even within what seems to be a homogeneous population, functional differences do exist. Table 4 outlines eleven classes of activities among which managers (senior, middle level) and professionals distribute their time. This distribution is broad enough to suggest that the "average" is a meaningless measure.

The software may have to be specialized even for secretarial jobs

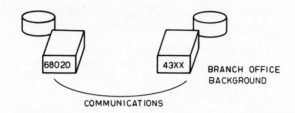

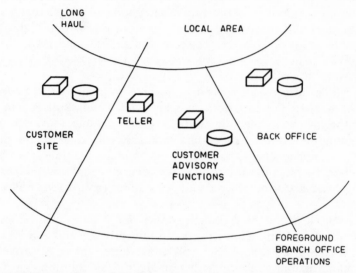

FIGURE 2. The need for data communications software and hardware.

because secretaries too are classified as senior or executive, junior, and typists. The daily secretarial activities shown in Tables 5 and 6 give us a representative distribution. The basic frames of reference should be studied locally by job to establish the relevant statistics within a given environment.

Such studies preparatory to establishing the universal WS are both urgent and important. The transition from the "old" (which means *current*) to the *new* technology will hit the office by 1987, and it will bring a higher level of quality and sophistication to the business office.

- *The transition will be based on communications,* and great care must be exercised to assure that the communications chores are carried out properly.

- *The transition will also be based on quality workstations.* By 1987, present-day engineering quality WSs will be on the secretarial desks. That will be necessary in order to handle documents. Document processing is the cornerstone of office automation.

16

TABLE 4   Job-oriented daily activities of managers and professionals

| | | Percent of available time | | |
Activity	Rounded average	Senior manager	Middle manager	Professional
Meetings:				
Scheduled and unscheduled	16.1	27.6	13.4	7.2
On the telephone	13.5	16.8	12.3	11.3
Writing	11.9	3.8	14.2	17.8
Filing, searching, retrieving	10.4	5.9	12.1	13.1
Reading	9.7	10.5	9.9	8.7
Traveling	7.3	13.1	6.6	2.2
Calculating	5.9	2.3	5.8	9.6
Time with secretary (incl. dictating)	5.0	8.8	4.7	1.4
Mail handling	4.6	6.1	5.0	2.7
Planning and time scheduling	4.4	4.7	5.5	2.9
Other activities*	11.2	0.4	10.5	23.1
	100.0	100.0	100.0	100.0

* Wait time distributed to different projects and equipment-oriented tasks.

The developments of which we are talking make the workstation a *total information system.* There is no longer a need for distinct word processors, quotation terminals, inquiry terminals, and communications terminals. Nor is there any other machine which functions like a personal computer for the manager, the professional, and the secretary. But note this well: The effort can be successful only if the company adopts a *philosophy of universal development.*

The system should be managed and fed with text, data, voice, graphs, and images for the whole organization, and not just for certain offices.

- Either it is a good idea or it isn't.
- If it is not a good idea, why do it?
- If it is a good idea—and we can really leverage the productivity of our sales, manufacturing, and engineering forces—then we should do it across the board.

We should also provide everybody with hands-on experience with PC equipment. We should simulate the office environment, provide very specific scenarios, calculate the workloads, and streamline procedures and methodology.

TABLE 5 *Daily secretarial activities*

Activity	Available time, %*
Typing	36.0
On the telephone	12.8
Sorting, filing, searching	12.2
Mail handling	8.2
Copying, duplicating	8.1
Reading and proofreading	5.8
Taking dictation	5.5
Conferring with principals	4.3
Writing other than typing	3.0
Envelope handling, pickup, delivery	3.5
	100.0

* Not including wait time. There is, furthermore, an average of 65 minutes pause per day (personal allowances and so on) not reflected in these statistics.

In summary, the universal WS will offer electronic mail, word processing, calendar management, decision support, report writing, and telephone communications. All functions must be available from each personal computer, and each PC must be linked to local area and long-haul networks.

The software can be customized for end user or department through definable functions that create commands to bypass menus and modify services to reduce the number of keystrokes required. The system should let the user go to another function without disrupting the task in process. The user should be able to use a help menu or take a telephone message and return to the document being edited without discontinuities in any one of the jobs underway.

TABLE 6 *Use of copies*

Purpose of copy	Amount, %
Straight archiving*	47.3
Internal usage (same building)*	24.2
Internal usage (other buildings)†	13.5
External usage†	15.0
	100.0

* To substitute for the original through interactive retrieval
† To substitute for the original through electronic mail

What Constitutes Machine Capacity?

One of the most elusive computer subjects is machine capacity. Not only are there no precise units of measurement but a distinction between physical and logical characteristics should be made. Therefore, I would rather use the term *units of reference* to help define machine capacity. In a physical sense, the top five units of reference are:

1. *Millions of instructions per second* supported at the microprocessor level.
2. *Bits per word* with a distinction to be made between the arithmetic-logical unit and internal data transfer. The BPW also impact on the ability to address a larger memory.
3. *Megabytes of memory*, which has to do with both the central (random access) memory and the auxiliary memory typically supplied by hard disk.
4. *Bits per second* of internal data transfer, usually measured in kilobits or megabits. This unit is also employed with networks, whether local, metropolitan, or long-haul.
5. The picture element, or pixel, is a measure of the resolution of the screen, which is the most common input/output device in an office automation environment.

Although the above five are the most important units of reference, they are not the only ones. System design plays a key role in available capacity, and that is true also of technical details such as microcoding and the use of *cache*. The latter is a very high speed central memory that matches the speed of the processor. It interfaces between the larger random access memory and the arithmetic-logical unit, and it is nonaddressable by the programmer.

There are also logical, hence software-based, units of reference. The five most critical are:

1. The computer *operating system*, which runs the machine and manages its resources.
2. The *programming language* in which the applications software is written—particularly the user-friendly, high-productivity fourth generation of programming languages.
3. The *database management system*, which defines, manipulates, accesses, and administers the information elements in the database.
4. The *network architecture* and command structure, which assure that all the attached devices can work together as an aggregate.

5. The *user-friendly interfaces* including icon presentation, menu selection capability, prompts, help screens, and easy to learn and remember commands for interaction with the information resources.

Such units of reference are helpful to know and use. If taken as an aggregate, they can be reasonably accurate, but no single one is entirely precise. In this, as in most cases with advanced technology, the bottom line is money, and the choice lies in how to spend the money among competing units of reference and application ends.

Technical Notes

By definition, a *computer* is an electronic device that can be programmed to store, retrieve, and process data. Originally its primary components were vacuum tubes; then they were transistors; now they are minuscule silicon chips: *microprocessors* and storage devices. What tubes, transistors, and chips have in common is the capacity to store and manipulate *bits* (*b*inary dig*its*)—the raw material of information whether text, data, graphics, or voice. Bits are either 0s or 1s, usually combined in octets, or *bytes*. The easiest way to think of bytes is as the electronic equivalents of the characters found on a typewriter keyboard.

The computer stores, retrieves, and processes bits or bytes—which are therefore the commonest unit of measurement of machine storage capacity. How the computer operates on bytes is determined by the *software*, which comprises two broad classes of computer *programs:* basic software and applications software.

Basic software includes the operating system, which is selected by the computer manufacturer and which tells the microprocessor how to do its housekeeping job. It provides for communication with the user by means of a *programming language* such as Pascal, C, Basic, Fortran, Cobol, or PL/1. Also, and increasingly, it includes communications routines and database management capabilities.

Applications software includes all the programs to do the things that were the reason or reasons for buying the computer: to communicate with databases and other PCs, send and receive electronic mail, do lengthy computations, work on spreadsheets, create graphics, write letters and reports, or even play games.

Both kinds of software operate on the *hardware*, which in the case of the personal computer includes the evident screen or monitor, the microprocessor, central memory, hard disk, floppies, keyboard, and a printer. A *central processing unit* (CPU) is built around the microprocessor(s). The *central memory* is specified as 64, 128, 256, or 512 Kbytes. You will see references to *floppy disks*, or floppies, and *hard disks;* the differences are in construction, storage capacity, access time, reliability, and cost, and not in function. You may also see references to *laser disks;* again the differences are in construction, operation, and very large storage capacity.

The auxiliary memory is supremely important. It is the means of building a *database,* an aggregation of information so organized that it can be accessed, displayed, printed out, modified, and supplemented as needed. How it is organized is, naturally, determined by a software program for *database management.* Databases now contain not only data but also text, images, graphics, and digitized voice.

If personal computers are to serve effectively as workstations, they must be connected together to permit intra- and interoffice communication. Connections can be made by *local area networks* (LANs), which are effective over distances ranging from 980 feet (300 meters) to 6.2 miles (10 kilometers). They differ in many fundamental ways; for example, they may use pairs of wires as the telephone does, coaxial cable as in cable TV, or optical fibers.

In addition to communication between PC workstations, a LAN can be used to access a common database, such as a supermicro, mini, or mainframe computer, and *download* information from it. During that process, other demands on the LAN may be made by other workstations. They are dealt with according to a *protocol,* which can be defined as a rule of conduct or procedure to be observed by all workstations for the exchange of information bytes or *packets* between workstations. All this depends on following a set of principles that, like the principles of reasoning, are called *logic.* Communication between devices is possible only when the logical constructs and methodology characterizing the use of computer equipment are *shared.*

An *interface* helps link devices, parts of a device, and/or software. It connects two unlike things such as the computer and one of its peripherals.

A technical note about *windowing* is deferred until Chapter 2, and notes about *expert systems* are deferred until Chapter 7.

CHAPTER 2

The Product Is Information

The evidence of authority seems to prevail over the authority of evidence.

JEAN BRUN

One of the major features of business and industry today is the burgeoning demand for what the office produces: *information.* That demand is accelerating, and efforts by information professionals to satisfy it are falling short of expectations.

The office is nothing more than an extension of the human mind. It is an intelligence machine. If we want to make the machine run smoothly, we must first find how it works by asking the right questions. That is more important than the equipment we will get.

Since 1982 we have seen an extraordinary growth in the use of personal computers (PCs) to provide managers and professionals with information that is not readily available from traditional sources. Handled through personal computing, enriched with vast communications capabilities, fed through databases, and formatted in graphics and color, information has become a more powerful tool than ever before.

The basic trend in advanced office technology is to put PC capabilities in the hands of the end users. Personal computers have now brought the equipment selection and purchasing decision down to the user's level. That is a development with far-reaching implications for how best to manage information technology.

As 5 years of practice helped to document, the users have much clearer objectives than computer professionals ever had. *Their goal is to employ automated tools to improve their ability in communicating, databasing, and computing.* For the first time, managers are taking charge of computers and communications. They believe that office automation has created an environment of change within their corporate structures.

- In many instances, these changes have produced immediate benefits.
- In others, new problems have arisen. The solutions to those problems have greatly improved managerial control over workflow and led to higher managerial productivity.

Almost every executive would like to have a PC or intelligent terminal which, at the touch of a button, would produce up-to-date reports on the status *and future* of the organization. And so the widely publicized problems associated with the proliferation of PCs have underscored the need for a corporate information policy.

Breadth, Potential, and the Computer-Management Gap

The top priority in exploiting the breadth and potential of advanced office systems is to provide everyone who works in the office, from the chief executive officer down to the lowest mangement level, with new tools and new techniques. Unlike data processing, advanced office systems put the results of technology in the hands of nonspecialists. The systems allow the users to decide how facilities are to be used. It is up to management to direct the systems' purpose in the office. The overall aim should be to enhance intellectual capabilities.

At the same time, there is increasing interest in recognizing office automation (OA) as an extension of data processing (DP) toward the end user. Products and services include:

- Computers
- Software
- Data communications
- Database management systems
- Micrographics
- Facsimile equipment
- Electronic mail systems

- Word processing
- A large number of peripherals

In a world of converging technologies, organizing around a specific line such as data processing, telecommunications, or word processing is no longer relevant. Since the forward thrust of technology is that of providing capabilities to users, technology-based organizations should be structured in response.

More than anything else, *office automation is information management.* The real payoff in office automation does not come from automating individual tasks; it comes from linking a series of components to allow information to flow freely in many forms. This is consistent with the definition of OA as integrating:

1. Personal computing
2. Business planning through spreadsheets
3. Business graphics
4. Decisional support software
5. Expert systems
6. Document handling
7. Communicating with public databases
8. Electronic message systems
9. Voice mail
10. Networking of all office equipment to the mainframe

For the mid-1980s information management technology means, first of all, *interactive solutions:* The user guides the technology to do the information handling the *user* wants.

Second, the technology rests on *multifunctional approaches.* It assists in many different tasks that involve information transfer: computer conferencing, report presentation, and financial evaluation.

The third feature is *distributed architecture.* The system makes use of mainframes, minis, micros in any combination to serve the end user's purposes.

Developments have compelled information managers to reexamine organizational approaches. Most of them found themselves totally unequipped to handle the PC explosion and had to scramble to catch up. During the past few years, the *traditional* DP and office specialists have spent their time defending their turf rather than determining how best to cope with future organizational needs. They have failed to realize that the user community, increasingly knowledgeable and active, will not wait for them.

The computer-management relationship of 30 years standing is now reversing—to the discomfort of the computer professionals. Many DP specialists retreat behind their mainframes and fragile multidrop lines and try, beyond all reason, to discourage users from personal computing.

Another major concern is that the business community is ill-prepared to manage this conversion to an information economy. The office, where all these changes are taking place, is the least well-managed element in any corporate enterprise. Sophisticated management practices are rarely found in the office.

Most offices are not organized to manage information, produce it, and distribute it in a way that is meaningful. That directs senior management to the heart of the problem: the need for new images and imaginative solutions. The pressure grows day by day to reorganize technology-based entities, make them more responsive to technology trends, and tune them to user needs. With the advent of computer-based tools for the office, we are finally beginning to see the profound impact that office technology can have on the individual office worker.

To reduce administrative costs, many chief executive officers (CEOs) choose to upgrade the communication and control capabilities. Because managers and professionals in any office account for about 75 percent of all office costs, economic gains in increasing office performance can be dramatic.

In another reversal of past trends, organizations that have lost their competitive advantages often become the pioneers in introducing new technologies. To catch up with, if not surpass, aggressive competitors who are gaining in share of market, many of these organizations look to state-of-the-art computers and communications to give them renewed vigor and competitiveness. There is plenty of opportunity for doing so. Among financial and industrial organizations, information:

1. Is, for the most part, not managed
2. Is available in overabundance or not at all
3. Is seldom timely and complete
4. Is provided at a cost that cannot be determined

In 1984 the approach to information management was based on yesterday's concept and technologies; the image of what could be done with current media dated back three or four decades. Yet, every 6 months something very significant happens to change the way we look at the workplace. The best projection is that this will continue to happen in some measure until the middle 1990s. The PC impact is felt everwhere:

1. It provides a track for new capabilities—spreadsheets, word processing (WP), electronic mail (Email), and so on.
2. It is single-user-oriented and simple and easy to use (as long as we stay on the PC level).
3. It exhibits communications-intensive features in linking with private and public databases as well as with other PCs.
4. It offers very good supports, graphics, color, resolution, and voice I/O.

Those capabilities are superior to any that mainframes and minis have been able to offer. PC-based intelligent workstations feature first-class integrated software, multiple windows, advanced graphics, and voice recognition and synthesis. The impact of advanced software will be widely felt. Before the end of the decade open-ended organizations will stop supporting host services other than databasing and data communications (DB/DC).

Improving the Span of Management Control

A vital task of management is that of building organization and structure. It involves three activities. The first is determining the kind and extent of specialization that is to be present in the work of a business unit. The second is undertaking the allocation of authority, responsiblity, and accountability for the performance of the specialized work. The third is striving for coordination in the work to be done within a well-defined environmental perspective. That is exactly where a properly designed information system can support management in an able manner.

To properly define the functions within an organization—authority, responsibility, and accountability—and thereby contribute to the accuracy which should characterize it, management typically examines the span of control and the environmental interfaces to be established. This work is done according to the principles of management, which involve six key functions:

1. Forecasting
2. Planning
3. Organizing
4. Staffing

5. Directing

6. Controlling

In the bottom line, however, the act of management consists essentially of directives and controls.

From the standpoint of directives, there is no narrow limit to the number of people to whom an executive can issue an order. But there is a limit of control. The *span of control* is an underlying principle of business organization. Its limits are determined by other spans such as:

- Knowledge
- Time
- Energy
- Personality
- Information systems support

In its narrower sense, the span of control refers to the maximum number of subordinates who may be placed under the jurisdiction of one executive who is immediately superior to them.

Citibank has been successfully using information systems to enlarge the span of control. From a recent meeting I record that, from an early 1970s average of 1:5, the span of control has now reached 1:7. The next goal is 1:8. What this means in terms of management is detailed in Table 7. With seven layers of supervision we can reach 78,000 people

TABLE 7 *Effects of a broader span of control on the layers of an organizational structure*

Organization layers	People commanded when span of control* is		
	5	7	8
1	5	7	8
2	25	49	64
3	125	343	512
4	625	2,401	4,096
5	3,125	16,807	32,768
6	15,625	117,649	262,144
7	79,125	823,543	2,097,152
8	390,625	5,764,801	
9	1,953,125		

* To command, say, 2 million people, you need at least nine organizational layers with a span of control of five people, eight layers with a span of seven, and seven layers with a span of eight.

28

if five managers depend on a superior, 823,000 if the span is seven, and over 2 million if the span is eight.

A greater span of control has important side effects in making the organization leaner and more able to respond to changing situations. There are, as well, significant cost advantages to be obtained. Remember, however, that computers and communications are the catalyst. A good job of cutting fat will be done if the preparatory work is thorough and clear goals are set. For example, it is essential when enlarging the span of control—and thus reducing organizational fat—to choose able assistants and keep them well trained at all times.

It is also quite proper to emphasize that, within the span-of-control perspectives, the *span of knowledge* is a most important factor which considerably extends, affects, or modifies the levels of management. The ancient maxim that "knowledge is power" has particular force in managerial activity.

Knowledge, time, and energy together define the *span of attention.* The human brain is able to pay attention efficiently and effectively to relatively few items at a time. The greater the knowledge, personal energy, and time saved by the able use of information systems, the broader can be the span of attention of an executive.

Less definite in its nature than time and energy, and more difficult to analyze than knowledge and control, is the *span of personality.* Personality has been defined as the part of character that is effective in influencing other people. Favorable influence is, very evidently, to be sought after.

However, although a manager may have both the personality and the knowledge to master a wide span of control, his or her contribution to the growth, survival, and profits of the organization can be limited by defective, ill-designed, or under-capitalized information systems. Hence there is the need to become a leader in the computer and communications field and to stay on the right track.

We can learn how to exploit computers and communications more skillfully when we appreciate their strengths and encounter their limits, learn to use their strengths to our advantage, and evaluate how to behave when against their limits. We can be successful in those respects only when we stay slightly ahead of the state of the art.

Office System Direction

The office system is evolutionary. There is not going to be a day when *the* office system will be pronounced "ready" and "good for all." Office systems technology both leads and follows customer implementation. The vendor cannot ignore user requests, nor can the user forget about the investment made so far. Hence, there is *the need to create an architecture.*

An office systems architecture provides for continuity, one of the key benefits to be derived from an architectural solution. Furthermore, the architecture must support:

- Long life cycle
- Configuration flexibility
- Open vendor capability

Since it is unlikely that any single vendor will be able to meet every requirement of an organization, management should follow an open vendor policy. It should particularly call for selecting the manufacturers who have the expertise to integrate their systems with the equipment already installed and thereby more completely meet the information and business needs of the organization.

Vendors steadily introduce new systems, and users steadily define richer requirements based upon the new levels of knowledge they have gained from system installations. It is therefore most important to forecast the next cycle in an implementation and recommend strategies for an able response to the evolving requirements.

Just as important is a policy of integrating equipment from multivendor sources of supply. Only by pursuing this policy can effective use be made of a broad range of offerings and advantage be taken of truly new equipment on the market. Further, integration of diverse sources of supply and/or equipment is a necessity because different departments have different equipment needs. Secretarial and managerial requirements will not be met with the same software.

A companion policy is to see to it that system components are, by their design, able to communicate even if used alone. As experience accumulates, the organization will realize the need for interconnection. *From this capability comes the notion that we can turn the workstation into a window to the outside world.* This calls for information transfer through transparent connectivity, and it includes:

- Software and hardware
- Data communication protocols
- User interface

Connectivity requirements led to the need for compatibility of both text and data format and vehicles. The service must translate information to a recognizable format, handle revisable from/to forms, and know what to do with the information once delivered.

The information service must also be dynamic and expandable. *The value of an office system goes up as the number of participating users increases.*

Unless it is properly planned and proceeds with good speed, however, it can take several years to reach a critical mass. Furthermore, integration difficulties may delay the effort. They too should be studied in advance. In terms of office systems requirements:

1. The foremost need for the 1980s is the ability to integrate all information types: voice, data, text, image, and graphics.

2. The second need is for consistency in user interface across different types of equipment and in spite of the sometimes conflicting needs of users.

3. The third need is for a consistent format in the text and database, including message and file interchanges.

For information elements (IE) and information functions within the network, we need directories. These directories must be able to operate across systems. We must also develop network management capability to assure that, at the user level, implementation is not dependent on the operator and the system can still work when something goes wrong. This will further enhance the exploitation of the open-ended facilities embedded in an intelligent workstation (WS).

The strategy I have described fits nicely with the goal of providing the user with access to authorized text and data and the ability to exchange information. These should be basic objectives of an office system. Not only is an office system not just word processing as it is thought to be but the future is even further away from WP. The future includes:

- Linguistics
- Signal processors (image, audio)
- Very fast microprocessors
- Windowing and window editing

Figure 3 exemplifies windowing by presenting five *paving stones* * on the same large-size, high-resolution video screen: voice annotation, text, data, image, and graphics. But we have to be very careful with implementation. We can automate bad practices as well as we can automate good ones. Success is not automatic.

While we increase the cost in product technology there may be no corresponding increase in management productivity—unless the right preparatory work and training was done. Training can make the difference between success and failure, and results will be the best where

---

* The word "tile" is avoided because "tiling" is one of the two competing windowing technologies; the other is multiple window overlays with the higher one being the active one.

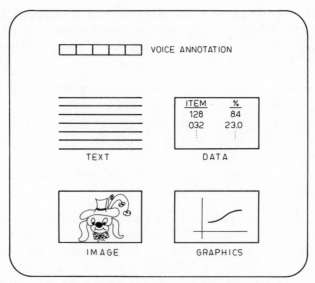

FIGURE 3. Five office system paving blocks on the same large-size, high-resolution screen.

there is the highest human intelligence. *Integrating mediocrities gives us nothing more than integrated mediocrities:*

Why should we not invest one-half day per month for an application that can save 3 days of work per month while it also improves our decision-making ability?

Furthermore, specific solutions are necessary. Something that is equally good for everything is not worth a damn for anything. Specific requirements call for specific solutions; and when the conditions are changed, new requirements must be studied.

Approaching the Systems Study

Offices, regardless of their size or the nature of the business, are information centers where efficient management of information flow is vital. The way in which an organization collects, organizes, stores, retrieves, and disseminates information will often determine overall success of the organization.

The first vital step toward an effective system is analysis of the office function. That is, incidentally, true of *any* project when the aim is to introduce computers and commmunications in a successful way. Some of the critical questions are:

1. Is the underlying structure of the office appropriate for OA?
2. How inherently flexible is the current structure?
3. How are the various functions interrelated?
4. How easy is it to interrupt one task and pick up another?
5. How well can the system support a task that may have been suspended in midstream?

Knowing that the crucial element in making an office system acceptable is the user interface,

6. How will the new system handle its exchange with people?
7. Are there different ways to interact with the system?
8. Is the interaction easy, forgiving, and self-explanatory, with help and prompt functions?
9. Is response time consistently good?
10. Is the system able to grow topologically in number of functions and users as demand expands?

Many aspects of office automation have developed from computing, and others have developed from word processing. However, the skills needed to analyze problems with advanced technology are not the same as those needed with DP and WP. A valid methodology is quite important, because the organization must carefully analyze the implementation program needed to develop and properly utilize the available technology and knowledge.

Training has already been mentioned. Included in that effort are the skills necessary for the analysis, design, and justification of office automation systems. Equally important, but not so often appreciated, is the need to teach analysts and designers in how to train the end user. And, of course, another integral part is the training of the end user. Users generally do not sit down at a computer and immediately work with spreadsheets or create complex documents. System training and adequate documentation are critical to the successful introduction of office automation. Support and training in methods should be tailored to the user's level: management, professional, or clerical. Learning techniques must be carefully explored. Typically, the company successful in OA will be dedicated to training users.

It is equally important that the new system analysis groups for OA be staffed with professionals who are service-oriented. They should be people who not only possess a good degree of business knowledge but also have the ability to show a manager how the WS relates to managerial problems.

Ideally, these new system analysts and designers should be business school graduates—or operating department people—who speak management's language. One of the biggest problems we face is convincing the line manager that the microcomputer can be a decision support tool when linked to a large database. It takes someone with a solid understanding of the end user's problems to do that. The system analyst should also make sure the system under development allows users to expand the scope of their work. Doing *better work* should be the goal.

To obtain quality as well as productivity, the system analyst must study the wide range of occupations the office comprises and how they are integrated. Office automation can offer a broad spectrum of solutions based on a diversity of new machines. As already stated, integrating those machines is the analyst's challenge.

A thoughtful analyst is careful in approaching the computerization of the workplace and first determines the functions that already exist in the organization. By reorganizing the work environment, the analyst can increase efficiency and cut costs.

Two prominent features of the work environment are the location of people and functions and the key volume indicators. Their proper identification should first show the major activities occurring in a department; *then* it should provide measurements; and it should include qualitative descriptors. Poor automation is to be expected if the right methodology is not followed. Computers and office equipment will not improve a bad situation; they will only make it worse.

In every successful human activity there are priorities to be observed. The requirements of the business must be the driving force; then comes the clear definition of objectives and the way to meet them. Management should be deeply involved in this effort. Above all, *nobody should attempt to solve problems by throwing people, money, or computers at them*. Everybody should:

- Examine the problems in detail
- Propose solutions
- Document the solutions

A good methodology would start with the assumption that offices are not prepared to manage information; historically, information has not been treated as a corporate resource. Procedures have usually been haphazardly rather than rationally established. That is why many of today's offices, as they stand, are unfit to do the work assigned to them.

A great deal of effort will be needed to change that. Emphasis should be placed on fundamental studies. Nothing should be taken for granted. Otherwise, information management will remain an elusive objective.

The system analyst should be keen to streamline the paperwork. If done correctly, that can help cut costs and raise the corporate competitive position with a single investment. Paper forms can be replaced with:

- Electronic forms
- Source data entry
- Point-of-destination reporting

Computer printouts can give way to exception reports, color graphics displays, and online queries. Since paper will be replaced by computer-stored text, data, and graphs, it is proper to give this subject a great deal of attention.

Typically, in an office environment the database will be distributed. The concept of distributed database management systems (DBMS) is one of the most intriguing subjects in information management, and distributed software is required to turn that concept into reality. When a distributed database is installed, every step, from assessing the needs of end users to assigning data administrators, is crucial to its success. A carefully thought-out plan will see to it that, before installation is discussed, duties and responsibilities down to those of the last end user are clearly defined.

Providing both Quality and Productivity

The PC prospered because of management's frustration. Management wanted results and could not get them from central data processing. This is one of the cases in which frustration produces results.

The popular approach to OA is based on what machines can do. *The goal should be how an integrated system can provide both quality and productivity.* Productivity is the result of a deep personal drive to do something. It is a creative activity. That is also true of the quality of the work which we produce.

A recent study of two dozen Fortune 200 companies found that executives are the most important force in the growing use of integrated office systems. Significantly, these are organizations that made the strategic decision to position themselves ahead of competitors by the careful use of OA. That strategy pays dividends. These financial and industrial organizations, the study has established, have quickly become very large users of management workstations at the highest levels. In the process, they have made significant contributions to the mental productivity of the enterprises.

The modern office has access to advanced technologies which, if properly implemented, can result in improved productivity and increased revenues. Today's business world functions primarily on the collection, analysis, and use of our most valuable resource: information. To remain competitive, executives and staff are called on to make business decisions that are both cost-effective and based on timely and accurate information. That is why timely comprehensive information has become such a valuable commodity.

We have to start looking at white-collar productivity from an assembly line viewpoint. The bottom line is quality and service: *the customer's degree of satisfaction*. The *customer concept* can be applied at every step taken to produce a marketable product, and not just to the ultimate consumer. Services provide *added value*.

Although OA gear is necessary, the simple collection of equipment will not guarantee satisfaction of needs. Neither is its selection a straightforward walkthrough process. The OA industry has been plagued by an extraordinary number of unsuccessful products. Part of the difficulty in confronting a selection procedure is that there are few guidelines on which to rely. Theoretical design concepts have proved to be of little value.

We therefore need to explore the OA issues in a fundamental way to provide ourselves with some guidance for design evaluation. We can do so by returning to basic principles: What makes for a successful product? What does it take to choose one? How should we go about designing a flexible system? Which are the basic steps for a successful functional implementation?

We must, furthermore, appreciate that, as office automation matures, there is a need to integrate it with data processing, telecommunications, and other elements of the corporate information resource. Moreover, over a rather lengthy transition period, OA plans require coexistence of equipment from multiple vendors.

For these reasons systems integration has become a major obstacle to hurdle on the path toward a successful system. Integrating data and word processing requires adequate planning with emphasis on the human resources in an organization. These human resources should be able to:

- Establish the DP and WP overlap
- Identify how today's components provide the expanded support of the integrated office
- Plan for integration

Writing procedures, training, and evaluating the gradual development toward an integrated office are among the key issues which need to be addressed. A successful integration also calls for pilot programs able to reach some of their functions' critical masses. Prototyping is a good way to get experience prior to making significant decisions or starting projects that will take 3 to 5 years to complete.

System integration should be no barrier to further diversification and expansion. Distributed systems allow people to work in the most natural way: using remote database structures to provide dependable, timely service—which is locally supported through intelligent, multifunction workstations. Communications is an essential goal of OA. Systems should help people to generate ideas easily and share them with coworkers.

In summary, OA comprises a wide range of solutions, but such solutions should assure both expandability and integration:

- They should help in generating ideas.
- They should not stand in the way of further developments.
- They should be fully shared by all members of the organization under the prevailing authorization rules.

The future is incredibly exciting to a company which has a system strategy, high technology, competent people, and a high level of expectations. Each one of these features is vital to survival.

Let me also add this thought. *Very few people in their lives have the opportunity to participate in a revolution. Yet this is the challenging future of those who work in office automation and are able to face up to the developing opportunities.*

Technical Notes

If the personal computer is reduced to its essential, which is the microprocessor, the *peripherals* are just about everything else: monitor, disk drives, printer, plotter, badge reader, passbook printer, and so on. They are, typically, the *input output,* and *storage units.* One of the virtues of the LAN is that some of the peripherals (disks, printers) can serve several workstations at the same time.

That introduces the *system architecture,* which provides a unifying, coherent, logical structure within which to integrate devices that are not necessarily compatible by their nature. Such devices may be minicomputers or mainframes and their terminals, personal computers, gateways to communications networks, or free-standing databases. The architecture should also provide flexibility for further expansion.

Windowing is a computer capacity that permits the user to access and display on the screen two or more kinds of information (from the same origin or from different origins) at the same time. The technique is similar to that of the familiar split screen of television sportscasting. Windowing offers the computer user a means of comparing two or more subjects of interest and of doing so without interrupting an activity then underway. The activity may or may not be related to the subjects in the windows.

A *text and database* is an organized, orderly collection of information elements designed in an applications-independent manner to serve data and word processing purposes. It includes all files stored in an organized, planned fashion, and it constitutes a storehouse of information about all corporate data for any purpose. It is a corporate resource. A *file* is a unit of information, variable in length, that is identified by a filename under which it is stored on disk and by means of which—and *only* by means of which—it can be retrieved. It can be protected with a password and authentication.

CHAPTER 3

Machines to Assist the Human Mind

*In this world, it is very important to understand
things 15 minutes before somebody else.*

OLD PROVERB

In 1642, Blaise Pascal (then 19 years old) made an automatic device
that could add or subtract with the turning of little wheels. In that same
century, Gottfried W. Leibnitz added the power of multiplication and
division.

Leibnitz also proposed to the papal envoy to China that the binary
number system be used to convert the Chinese to Christianity. He said
that through this system one could logically demonstrate that, from
nothing and the one true God, everything proceeds. This was his expecta-
tion for a system that became the basis of all computers.

In the nineteenth century, Charles Babbage designed the differential
engine. Halfway through the same century, while working on the theory
of probability, George Boole developed the basic laws which made the
binary system an established mathematical discipline. During the same
time frame, the Industrial Revolution was in full swing. In Great Britain
it was based on steam power and coal. The second industrial revolution,
in about 1900, was based on chemical and electrical industries in Germany.

Although we have preserved historical monuments of antiquity, the Middle Ages, and the Renaissance, that has not been true of the factories and products of the Industrial Revolution. A precious historical heritage has been lost, but the mathematical basis has not been. The roots put down by Pascal, Leibnitz, Babbage, and Boole led to the third industrial revolution or, more precisely, *the first knowledge revolution,* which is now underway. It is based on the microchip and, eventually, the regenerative power of genes.

The design of the world's first computer is disputed by many, but existing evidence is that Konrad Zuse was the pioneer in the 1930s in Germany. He was followed by Lord Bowden in England and Eckert and von Neumann in the United States. In 1939, AT&T's George Stibitz built a computer-like device and showed how it could work over telephone wires. It was the earliest display of data processing and data communications (DP/DC).

Created at the University of Pennsylvania, the first American computer ENIAC (Electronic Numerical Integrator and Calculator) weighed 30 tons and contained 6000 switches, 10,000 capacitors, 70,000 resistors, and 18,000 vacuum tubes. It had a mean time between failure (MTBF) of 7 minutes. Today, the Intel 80286 microprocessor integrates 130,000 transistors, or roughly 20,000 gates, on a chip and has an MTBF of several thousand hours.

Systems that used to weigh 30 tons are now packed on printed-circuit boards (PCBs). Those which used to be on boards are now on chips. As the computer itself is reduced to pieces of silicon, computer and semiconductor manufacturing tend to merge. That is true of computers and communications also. Advance of technology underlies this trend. Pricing advantages are gained not only through high-volume production but also through steady integration. Originally made from over 200 component parts, the IBM PC has been redesigned to reduce that number to 8.

The first microprocessor-based machine—the new breed of computers—appeared in 1975 and was marketed to hobbyists. Altair 8800 cost $395 in a kit form and $620 assembled. Soon thereafter some forty competitors jumped into the market. Of the forty, only a few remain; Apple, Tandy, and Commodore are the best known. Others, like Heath, changed into marketing chains. Altair disappeared.

Using Intelligent Machines

The world seems to be filling up with the new applications of computers and communications: personal workstations, microprocessors, microfiles, optical disks, interactive services, and local networks. We are experiencing the integration of word processing and data processing. Everywhere we look we can see innovative approaches to computer applications. At their core are microcomputers, which are now commonly called personal computers (PCs).

Actually, however, the power of the PC lies not in hardware, but in software. The emphasis of the information system discipline has changed. For the 1980s, databasing and data communications will be the most widespread tasks in computing.

No matter how the user thinks of his information, ultimately it will have to be stored on some medium then retrieved, updated, transported and made available for man-information communications purposes.* Speaking on investments in intelligent workstations, Admiral Inman† aptly remarked: "The future depends on providing the most automated working environment possible."

Microcomputers and semiconductor technology now allow the distribution of computing resources at the personal level. But the potential of this new style of personal service can be attained only when all elements are connected together in a high-speed, tightly coupled aggregate. Resources must be shared by thousands, even millions of users.

This points to *new directions* for the end of this decade. Now and for the coming years advanced information technology means:

1. **Interactive Solutions.** Users guide hardware and software embedded in their equipment to do the information handling *they* want.

2. **Multifunctional Approaches.** The technology assists many different tasks that involve information handling: database management transparent to the user, electronic mail, computer conferencing, report presentation, financial evaluation, and integrated tools.

3. **Distributed Architectures.** The system makes use of micros, minis, and mainframes, in any combination, to assist the end user. By bringing computer and communications power to the desk, we amplify the user's mental capabilities.

Now more than ever we must appreciate that we should use the tools we have made to propel us forward. We should not fight technology;

---

* In 1948 Norbert Weiner, a prominent mathematician, gave the name "cybernetics" to his pioneering study of communications between human beings and machines. In a popular work on the subject he spoke of the man-machine interface. With an apology to those who see something sexist in such a generic use of the word "man," I have retained his terminology. "Information" has, however, become a better second term of the couplet.

† Chief executive officer of Microelectronics and Computer Development Corporation, America's spearhead into the fifth-generation computer system and the technologies of the next century.

we should use it. Fighting it is like jumping in front of a freight train.

We should also think ahead of our time and plan for what is coming next. We usually find that the very things we think we are not going to need become the necessities of the future. Shortcomings in planning and controlling the use of workstations for data access, decision support, and office automation at large incur heavy costs. That is true both in financial terms and in regard to the organization's human resources.

Planning the personal computer's implementation and supporting the end user's needs are tasks very different from those performed by classical data processing in a traditional environment. The mission is complicated by the fact that training human resources—particularly the computer specialists—lags the technical developments in software and hardware.

It is therefore important that every organization face up to new policy requirements. Resources must be used to increase the information effectiveness of the firm—and thereby multiply manyfold the available human capabilities. This has not yet been a universal realization. All around the globe, sluggishness in applying available knowhow is a major reason for falling behind in state of the art, experiencing product obsolescence, delaying the necessary decision process, and losing control of the market.

The leaders of business and industry manage, consult, and educate against entrenched organizations. That has been so for ages. Now they can accomplish more in moving ahead with their times by applying the most advanced tools technology presents to them.

A basic fact of computers and communications is the advent of attractive cost/performance ratios. The microprocessor has made it possible to insert computing power virtually anywhere in a network. In that way, the site at which any particular function is performed has been made optional. At the same time, this flexibility has increased the emphasis on common protocols, data formats, and interfaces. Without this common ground, the opportunity to capitalize on new technologies is lost.

When computer power is installed at the workplace, the vital role of the human element becomes evident. An efficient information system depends on more than hardware and software. If a system is to work, we must consider the most important variable: *people*. The key questions are:

1. How do we manage our employees for highest productivity?
2. How do we establish workable, cost-effective solutions?
3. How do we program the machines at our disposal?
4. How do we select the software and hardware suited to our requirements?

Programming the computer has been one of the key preoccupations since the advent of stored program machines. The early efforts were at the machine level. Within a few years they were supplanted by symbolic (assembly level) approaches and they in turn, for the mass of the work to be done, by compiler-level programming languages. Fortran and Cobol are examples.

The change from the first to the second and then to the third generation of programming languages took place in the 1950s. Typically, these generations of languages were separated by 3 to 4 years in respect to commercial computer exploitation.

Then came a period of stagnation lasting nearly 25 years. There were, of course, developments, but there were no totally new ideas. Neither were there really effective programming tools. The art of computer programming had to wait until the early 1980s for major breakthroughs.

Although the implementation of computer technology depends on it, software has been the one area in which results have lagged. Increasingly, software development came to represent enormous costs in time, labor, and money.

Something had to be done to improve software development productivity. While software quality was being improved, the time needed to get it had to be minimized. It was also desirable to encourage end users to develop some of the programs they directly needed, which they could do in an easy way if the proper tools were available.

That means bringing forward new techniques for the design and manufacture of software—a goal realized with fourth-generation languages (4GL). A basic trend in that direction is developing. It will quicken as the demand for computers and communications services increases.

What the Knowledge Worker Needs

New programming languages are necessary to serve in an increasing range of applications and to provide the growing number of multifunctional characteristics that users expect from modern technology. We are now facing as never before a synthesis of functions. It includes data processing (DP) and databasing (DB), word processing (WP), and graphics integrated comprehensively with data communications (DC) and voice communications.

A most evident trend is toward integration of voice, text, image, and data communications, no matter what special characteristics these services had when they were originally devised (Figure 4). Information is a product marketed to office and home. Information technology will soon have social, political, and economic implications.

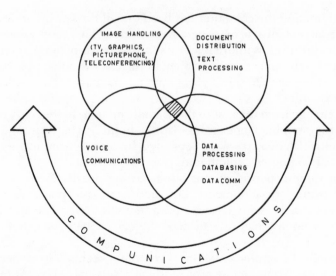

FIGURE 4. The evident trend toward integration of voice, text, image, and data communications called compunications.

The key to future corporate success is the ability to provide information *where* it is needed and *when* it is needed. A business firm, industrial concern, or financial institution must keep abreast of developments and assure technical leadership.

Management should identify new computing technologies and applications and analyze their impact. Redundant or incompatible solutions should be avoided by providing direction through sound system architecture. Users should be given implementation support, and the company as a whole will benefit from the acquisition of new technology (technology transfer). User expectations and perceptions are changing. We must learn to use computers and communications to make decisions that improve the way we do things.

Throughout the organization we must foster common solutions, protect investments from ever-decreasing product life cycles, and develop approaches responsive to business cycles. We must provide not only for flexibility but also for the capability to integrate all the services at our disposal.

One example of integration is the blending of voice and data communications with computers (*compunications*). This has become one of the vital features of modern technology, and it can be put to three main types of uses:

1. Replacing lengthy telephone calls
2. Substituting for short memos
3. Introducing new types of communications

Through *office automation* we must tie a wide variety of productivity-related products into computer-based systems for office work. Office automation perspectives range from the narrow view of bringing together copying, text input, text handling, and distribution to the broader view of providing the necessary infrastructure for data, text, image, and voice.

One of the basic chores of the office is mail preparation, distribution, reception, storage, and retrieval. Traditionally a manual operation (whether the letter is handwritten or typed), mail now becomes a prime target for change through the introduction of computers and communications in the office environment. Electronic mail (Email) already plays a leading role in business and private correspondence.

Most important, Email, computer conferencing, videotex, compunications, teletex, and office automation put to the test management's *will* to come to terms with the key problem of the 1980s: *physical and mental productivity in a service-oriented economy.* Not only do such developments greatly affect the workplace; they also shift our view to the decision-making structure as opposed to the operational and administrative orientation with which data processing and data communications have traditionally been concerned.

Decision support systems (DSS) emphasize the need for building databases to answer management questions or to work on problems as yet undefined and unstructured. With classical data processing, managers are overwhelmed by data yet are unable to obtain *relevant* information. High technology resolves this paradox.

We are just starting to design and implement interactive approaches, direct accesses to the database, softcopy solutions, and the use of graphs and color. We are definitely going to see a lot of color replacing black-and-white display terminals, and we are also going to see the integration of voice communications with other forms of information transfer.

Such systems aim to *augment the human intellect,* much as the invention of writing did, by providing new ways to store, retrieve, and manipulate text. They work at all stages of document production from composition to final display, operate on a whole system of documents rather than a single one, and are used *collaboratively*: once written, the text can be edited either singly or jointly with others.

This shift emphasizes the *knowledge worker* rather than the clerical worker. Word processing aids the secretary, not the executive; compunications aids both but most importantly the latter. As an increasing number of people are exposed to computers and programming, and at the earlier stages of life, technology will be enmeshed in the fabric of society.

The broad picture of the developments now underway can best be explained with graphs. Figure 5 positions high technology at the center of a broad array of activities including consumer electronics, bank engineering, office automation, voice, text, and data communications, data

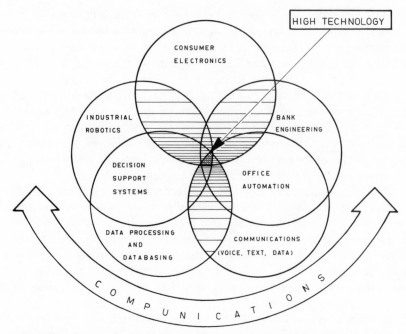

FIGURE 5. High technology is positioned at the center of a broad array of activities with a compunications foundation.

processing and databasing, decision support systems, graphics for management, CAD/CAM, and industrial robotics. The foundation of all is compunications.

Organizational studies and rationalization are basic prerequisite steps. The wrong approach to the implementation of new technology is to look at the productive units—whether office or boardroom—as complex communications systems without examining the existing communications paths between:

- The hierarchical layers of management
- User groups and system implementors
- Structural implications
- The operating environment

The right way to implement the new technology is to start with a perception: a framework within which we establish a coherent systems strategy based on gradual growth from a core user group and focusing on results to be obtained. One of the most important results is time management.

Time Management

During the 1960s, 1970s, and 1980s technological, economic, and social forces transformed our lives and altered the way we do things at the personal and corporate level. Perhaps none of the effects have been more dramatic than the realization that time is a vital resource.

The paradox of time is that nobody seems to have enough of it, yet everyone has all the time that's available. All of us have 24 hours a day, but time management is a question not of how many hours and minutes we have but of how well we utilize them.

Time is a unique resource. It cannot be accumulated like wealth, yet without it we can accomplish none of our tasks. Shakespeare said there are three things that don't return in life: an opportunity that has been lost, a word that has been spoken, and time that has passed by. We are forced to spend time whether we choose to or not, yet of all our resources it appears to be the least understood and the most mismanaged.

If the steam engine was the prime mover of the industrial age, *the clock is central to the postindustrial society. The computer is the information extension of the clock.* Actually, an orderly, punctual life, which made its first appearance in a monastery, is not natural to mankind. By now, however, the West has become so regimented by the clock as to approve the aphorism: *Time is money.*

In a prophetic book published by McGraw-Hill in 1955, *Principles of Management,* Harold Koontz and Cyril O'Donnell state:

> No one can vary the number of minutes in an hour.
>
> *If managers learn to live with the clock,* they will concentrate on the development of better and more flexible plans, and reduce the time lag between planning and execution.

Koontz and O'Donnell were professors of business administration at the University of California. They both had wide business experience prior to joining the faculty. Dr. Koontz was with Dr. Dietrich and Howard Hughes on the three-man board which ran the Hughes empire. Based on this experience, Koontz and O'Donnell advise:

> *Time is fast becoming the strategic factor in enterprise.*
>
> The rapid development of automation and the prospect of automatically controlled processes imply heavy costs for interruptions of any sort.
>
> One of the most important [issues] will be the time involved in planning, communication, and decision making.

At a premium is the ability to identify a problem quickly and deploy the organizational resources needed to handle it. When we evaluate such a performance, what should be the criteria? *Physical* and, more important, *mental productivity*, are at stake. The latter is a function of our ability to obtain the necessary information when we need it and in the way we want it presented.

A tremendous amount of creative ingenuity is available within the minds of most individuals if only a way can be found to tap it. Computer power should be directed toward that end, which suggests that information services should reach each and every workplace.

Computers and communications systems can help the manager, but they cannot provide motivation to do the job. All computer-based solutions depend on our having clear-cut procedural approaches. Here are some of them:

1. Commit yourself to clearly defined goals in planning your time and your budget.

2. Schedule a few minutes at the beginning of each day (and of each week) to review your program.

3. Write your goals and set priorities.

4. Once the priority list is prepared, the next step is to begin. (Rubinstein once said the hardest part of practicing the piano was sitting down at the keyboard.)

5. Recognize that the most notorious of all time wasters is preoccupation with side issues rather than the key subject.

6. Filter out the irrelevant. Do this by defining to yourself the precise purpose of a conversation, a meeting, a letter to be written, or a report.

7. Instead of having subordinates bring you problems, have them bring you the answers. *You* ask the questions.

8. Don't sit on projects; pass them along to people and delegate authority (with the corresponding responsibility and accountability).

9. Review and control your objectives. The environment is dynamic; your goals, and the means you have to realize them, may be changing.

10. Set up checkpoints to control the time, money, and people invested in a project—and handle each project as if your professional status depended on its success.

In planning time it is wise to keep a *time inventory* or log. A log can be astonishingly revealing of the vast amounts of time we all waste and motivate us to manage ourselves more effectively. We must set our goals for each day, write them down, and as the day progresses, record the results achieved. Here is where computer-based tools can be of help.

Superficially it might seem that the ten-step advice just outlined is alien to computer usage. It is not. Time can be managed ably by using computers and communications provided the necessary preparatory work is done thoroughly.

Personal computing tools help keep track of time. They serve as reminders, include prompts, provide an interactive scratchpad which can be reached from any point at any time. Communications link the personal computing facilities into one network of shareable resources. If properly used, compunications can help cut down time losses by handling voice, text, data, graphs, and images more effectively. But that does not alter human nature. A major role is still left for proper preparation and having the right spirit.

Time losses occur in slow starts, procrastinations, resistance to change, interminable discussions, disorganization, paperwork, overinvolvement in details and trivialities, fatigue, crisis, and team conflicts. The procrastinator induces crisis situations and tension. No computer can help sort out that mess. It is a *personal problem* that calls for organizational and procedural approaches.

Next to organization, the bottom line in implementing the latest advances in technology is savings in time and labor and therefore costs. That, quite naturally, requires capital investment, but there is plenty of room for improving the work being done in the office and thereby earning a good return on the investment.

In the United States today there is an average of only $2000 in capital investment in information machinery of all sorts to support each office worker; compare that with a $35,000 investment in equipment to support each agricultural worker on a fully mechanized farm. There is, however, at least $6000 of capital investment for each office worker in a modern, highly automated banking operation.

Simplicity and Integration

Time management is prerequisite to obtaining productivity gains. Apart from our ability to save and manage the vital resource which is time, three most important dimensions of productivity gains are:

- Completeness
- Power
- Simplicity

Simplicity comprises ease of learning and ease of use. It is heavily affected by integration. *Integration* means ease of moving among the various features of a product offering—making different components appear to be similar. That typically happens because the components actually use identical subroutines and common files.

According to a recent survey, the major factor inhibiting office automation is the incompatibility of hardware and software supplied by different vendors. Unlike the traditional, centralized data processing environment, where there is typically a single mainframe vendor, most office systems have evolved into multivendor affairs for a number of reasons.

As the cost of systems continues to plummet and the PC becomes the typical office system workstation, it is increasingly difficult to control what the end user purchases. Even if standardization occurs at the hardware level, software options proliferate.

With the increasing levels of automation of complex operations it has become rather common to find two or more display terminals on the same desk. They are there to access different systems at the same time. Such redundancy is costly for reason of:

- The terminals themselves
- The software interfaces necessary
- The communications capabilities that support the terminals
- Human usability
- Office space

It is increasingly important to secure greater generality in workstation capability and to fully streamline the system. There is no room for two terminals on a desk. One must do all the work. For instance, the availability of WP software for the personal computer makes employment of independent word processors unwise. Equally unwise is having separate terminals for electronic mail and a host of other applications. In brief, we should capitalize on software to make best use of the hardware's capabilities. Also, we should remember that products are convergent. *The PC can be—should be—an integral part of mainframe resources.*

As a growing number of terminals require online access to more and more database facilities, the importance of integration increases. This influences the design of entire information systems rather than just the communications or end user functions of a given implementation.

Online links should produce better text and data systems. They should open to the end user the vast horizons of database resources, but they should also protect the databases from unauthorized access. Policies and rules are important, but just because there are security rules does not mean they will be observed. There must be safeguards.

The need for constant communication between PCs and mainframes derives from growing information requirements. *Integrating these machines is our challenge.* The goal should be a *universal workstation optimized by function.*

- Secretaries need word processing capabilities.
- The factory manager must have inventories and schedules at fingertips.
- The broker wants market data.
- The manager requires planning tools.

The terminals do not need to be different, although they do have different requirements. The same WS should be installed for and employed by managers, professionals, and supporting staff. Software makes the difference. Successful implementation, however, requires that a whole infrastructure be created to support the computers and communications system in an able manner. *The product is evolutionary.* There is *not* going to be a day when solutions will be pronounced "final" and "good for all."

Systems technology both leads and follows user implementation, from which arises *the need to build an architecture.* A systems architecture provides for continuity. From continuity comes the notion that we can turn the workstation into a window to the outside world. Just as important is the realization that *the value of an office system goes up as the number of participating users increases.* But unless we plan properly and proceed with good speed, several years can be needed to reach a critical mass.

This can be said as a conclusion to this chapter: Resolving managerial and technical problems associated with the introduction of high technology is becoming the goal of an increasing number of companies. As a matter of principle, progressive firms pay more attention to the benefits to be obtained from that line of action than to possible failures in pursuing it.

Successful management responds to market needs and involves end users in the development of an innovation. Able management also appreciates that costs are hidden all over the so-called established approaches. We live in a time of rapid change, and we have to move fast even to stay where we were.

The intelligent workstation—which is to say the personal computer— becomes a desk-level extension of the mainframe and its database. The PC-based workstation, with decision support systems, spreadsheets, electronic mail, calendaring, and other facilities, is designed to enhance the job of the manager or the professional. *This is very important because most business people don't want to compute—they want to communicate.* Therein lies the challenge—the implementation with the greatest future. The product is information. Management-type applications provide added value; and that is what men of knowledge want: *value.*

Technical Notes

The *microchip,* or *integrated circuit,* is a miniaturization of hardware that once took up much greater amounts of space and required much greater amounts of labor to construct. A computer is, after all, an electronic device akin to, say, an intelligent television set, and the developmental histories are roughly parallel. Early, nonintelligent TVs had large numbers of wires painstakingly soldered to components, and so had the ancestors of personal computers, the mainframes of the 1950s. Wire circuits gave way to *printed circuits* formed by depositing conductive material on plastic laminate of the Formica type. Components were soldered to the printed circuits, sometimes by hand. Economy and space dictated a succession of shortcuts, and now both the components and their connectors are formed on tiny slices of silicon: the microchip.

Softcopy and *hardcopy* are different ways of having a presentation on video and printing (or plotting) on paper. One can be seen only on the screen; the other can be handled in a classical manner, although it is inadvisable to do so. Hardcopy is simply a printout.

CHAPTER 4

Office Automation: Facts and Fiction

The new empires are the empires of the mind.

WINSTON CHURCHILL

Since 1980, financial institutions and industrial concerns have engaged in projects involving office automation (OA). Initially such projects were primarily aimed at establishing goals and procedures, but today there is a body of knowledge with which to meet the earlier challenges.

One of the most persistent findings in OA applications derives from what was learned through 30 years of experience in data processing: *Information systems are a matter of culture, not of machines.* The closer the computer gets to the workplace, the more evident this basic principle becomes.

The second fundamental principle has to do with the setting of goals: *What do we want to achieve?* The primary objective of an OA project is productivity, and that divides into two main parts:

1. Mental or managerial productivity, which is by far the more valuable of the two

2. Manual, or secretarial and clerical, productivity

The secondary objectives are many; they range from escaping from the swamp of paperwork to the merging of data processing (DP) and word processing (WP) and the efficient handling of services involving voice, text, data, and images. Such objectives integrate nicely with the primary one of increased mental and managerial productivity if the right preparatory work is done. That is why such integration has become the main challenge. To start the study and implementation of OA the right way, we must:

1. Clearly understand at the outset what OA can do and what it cannot do
2. Set goals that are consistent with priorities and requirements
3. Establish a time plan for action
4. Provide the resources needed to meet goals and timetables
5. Present management with concrete results
6. Review, evaluate, and take corrective action
7. Assure user collaboration and proceed with the applications

The office of the future is not going to be created from any one device; many devices will work together. That is true of specialists also. Success will largely be based on four factors:

- An information plan that details what needs to be automated
- The proper knowhow
- The right selection of software and hardware
- The ability to define the multifunctional character of an office system

Ours is a paper-multiplication society: its reproduction process is based on paper. In fact, today we write less than we copy. We have to check this long-standing trend, use computers and communications to assist us at the workplace, and assure that better, more efficient work can be achieved in a unit of time. This is the real essence of office automation.

The Role of Communications

The heart of office automation is communication: We have to link office functions, and this puts emphasis on both local area and long-haul networks. Communications are necessary to link the main elements of the office together:

- Voice
- Text handling

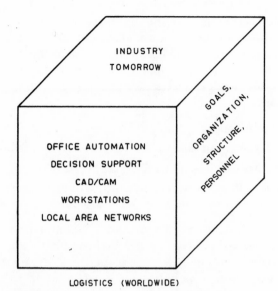

FIGURE 6. The requirements of tomorrow's industry.

- Data input
- Storage
- Retrieval
- Document distribution
- Visual display
- Hardcopy presentation

Tomorrow's industry will require increasing amounts of each of these elements, not piecemeal, but in an aggregate way; goals, organization, structure, and personnel will be conditioned by the quality and the availability of communications services. Office automation will integrate local area networks (LAN), computer-aided design and manufacturing (CAD/CAM) facilities, and decision support (DS) functions (Figure 6).

Systemwise, an OA project will involve communications capabilities, a computer complex, operating systems, text and database functions, access methods, network control programs, distributed resources, and multifunctional microprocessor-based terminals. The establishment of communications lines must be characterized by high-speed wideband facilities.

The ability to interconnect workstations (WS) through networks is fundamental to automating the office functions. But the communications network alone, whether local area or long-haul, is not enough. At the workstation level we need an intelligent terminal capable of functioning reliably, consistently, and in a way that is friendly to the user.

The characteristic WS of the late 1980s will be the personal computer (PC). The PC industry has emerged as one of the most dynamic and rapidly growing new-product areas in the history of our economy. Typically, PCs are:

- General-purpose
- Stand-alone, but also online to networks and databases
- Microprocessor-supported
- Able to fulfill the text and data processing requirements of individuals, small firms, and large-scale organizations

Although the existence of communications and of workstation facilities is generally known, one subject consistently escapes the attention of both management and the systems experts: If we want to get anywhere in office automation, it is important to get started, to do something. We should start immediately, since moving into the office of the future takes time for phasing in and adjustment. The sooner the transition is made, the sooner the return of higher productivity will show against the investment of:

- Time
- Effort
- Money
- Knowhow

But we should carefully plan the work to be done: Start small, introduce new technology on a department-by-department basis, and avoid any vast, companywide changes that will overwhelm employees. We should proceed gradually: Phase in new systems and services rather than introduce all of them in one indigestible lump and use OA technology only in areas where benefits are needed and will be immediately evident.

We should also integrate the new technology into our existing system and office structure: Present new equipment and services as aids to increased productivity, not as replacements for secretaries and support staff, and select an automated system that is compatible with the needs and preferences of management and employees.

Communications have a great impact which is not often recognized: Organizations are structured the way they are largely for reason of communications. That is why the integrated, high-capacity communications structure is about to effect changes in the way we live and work.

Geography is about to be put firmly into second place when we consider where and how to organize our productive resources. At least that is true for the information workers, who make up close to half our workforce. This is one of the fundamental factors to which management must pay more attention when doing long-range planning of communications resources. Such planning includes:

- Developing comprehensive strategies for migration to the computer and communications environment
- Integrating presently distinct facilities into one aggregate
- Moving from existing narrow-band, analog facilities to the inevitable wideband, all-digital facilities

The aggregate to which I refer constitutes the evolving message system. A microprocessor-based message system provides for the automatic distribution and receipt of information elements (IEs). An IE can be a brief memo, a phone call, a report, a drawing, a chart, or any other form of intelligence.

Voice, text, data, and image messages can be initiated, stored, or forwarded; a user should receive a signal on the WS screen when a new message is pending. This kind of *prodding* and *help* communication can greatly assist the man-information exchange.

Messages arriving at a WS are delivered to the recipient's electronic in-basket. From there, the recipient can read or listen to the mail, reply to it, forward it to another user, or copy it to a private library for future use.

An electronic directory is necessary for storage of user-defined lists. Such lists enable users to create their own customized directories so that they can quickly retrieve information that is routinely used. When equipped with autodialing hardware, the electronic directory can dial a selected telephone number. In an OA environment, electronic directories are much more valuable if they are so equipped. The extensive use of the corporate directories for internal calls, and that of the personal card index for external calls, suggests the need for autodial facilities to which voice mail and document distribution functions can eventually be delegated.

The more accessible a system becomes to its users, both source and destination, and the more features are automated, the greater the need for systems security. The security apparatus should provide the originator with the ability to specify system access based upon user requirements. In preparation for that, system management must assign users to specially designated classes. The exact scope of and the options available to each class must be determined.

Users will see on their WS screens only the information they need and are authorized to access: The most frequently used information should be the easier to access. To gain access, the operator must enter the ID; and to enhance security, a password also can be required.

Ease of use and security in operation are two of the pillars on which the OA system should be built. If they are not properly considered, the heralded technical benefits such as labor reduction, internal efficiencies, and increased managerial control will be illusions rather than realities.

- If we decide to automate, we should know the right questions to ask and be prepared to meet problems that can arise in the training and installation stages.

- If we have bits and pieces of the system in place, we should examine their function and performance to find the way to their integration without interrupting current service.

In neither case should we expect the new system to be an overnight success. Whether directed at managerial or secretarial productivity, office automation takes time and hard work to perfect. As so often in systems work, success depends on knowing how long it takes to succeed.

A Network Link

Emphasis has been put on communications as the element which helps create an aggregate by linking together the computer-based devices. Crucial to the success of office automation is the development of inexpensive and compatible local area networks to interconnect the electronic devices which are intended to improve managerial and/or secretarial functioning.

Without a LAN to allow word processors to communicate with office copiers, personal computers with electronic mail devices, and electronic filing devices with executive workstations, we will never be able to achieve commendable results. The component parts may be interesting; more often than not they will be expensive; but they will also be of limited usefulness if they are not integrated into an aggregate.

Local area networks are the means for moving information, connecting office equipment, and allowing various devices to function cooperatively. Given the need, and its basic simplicity, networking technology is progressing rapidly. As a Zilog executive remarked,

> Networks are the underpinnings of the office of the future. Without a network running through walls, floors, and ceilings, you can forget about implementing the electronic office.

To understand the impact of that statement, we have to look back at the evolution of WP concepts. During the 1970s, word processing machines evolved from the text-editing programs developed in the 1960s for changing, deleting, or adding parts previously saved in computer memory to create new documents. Computer-based word processors (WPs) revise and reprint typed documents quickly and efficiently; changes are made on a page; and a single keystroke causes error-free copies to be printed.

Letters, tables, reports, and manuals begin by being prepared on WPs, and the machines themselves have been more readily modified than earlier equipment to keep pace with growing demands. The word processors you choose should be PCs with WP software. Hence they should:

- Be microprocessor-based
- Use memory not only for document storage but also for greater flexibility in performing different operations
- Sustain high throughput both when entering and editing text and printing finished text
- Design-wise, be simple to use
- Embody the overall concept to replace a variety of dispersed equipment with one multifunctional unit

Incorporating the word processing function into the workstation has opened the way to a more competitive product. With microprocessors, intelligence can be programmed inexpensively throughout the system. And the key word is "nanosecond," which is to a minute what a minute is to 32 years.

Once again, end user orientation is fundamental to word processing. The machine should not resemble a computer so far as managers and secretaries are concerned. Users should learn no codes and have no contact with software. Instead, the display terminal should be used for prompts from the start-up, so that a complete set of built-in instructions guides users through every step of a job.

Typically, at start-up, a menu of operations should appear on the screen, along with a question about what activity the user wishes to perform. The latter replies by moving the screen cursor to the desired operation, then pressing the execute key. This brings up the next step, and another operation.

Word processors must have the capability to manage text and data and connect workstations (WSs) into a communications resource. The distributed WSs can be linked by a high-speed coaxial cable and a LAN architecture.

The communications rate should match the largest disk memory the system might need. A master microprocessor controlling the disk memory could thus communicate rapidly with every other memory in the LAN. With a rate of 4 MBPS (mega, or million, bits per second), for example, the transfer in the cable—about 2.6 ms/byte (microseconds per byte)—is much faster than the typical access time of 3.2 ms/byte for the hard disk and 32 ms/byte for the floppy disk. The LAN architecture should control resource management, disk memory, and system arbitration.

In this sense, it is feasible to integrate DP and WP at the WS level to share text and database and communications resources. Each WS should have just enough intelligence—a microprocessor and its own memory—to do most of the required job independently of any other station. All the LAN architecture has to do is:

- Handle the rear-end machine
- Actuate the gateway to other LANs
- Poll the stations or printers for requests for service

A basic advantage of a LAN-based WS is that the arrangement solves an industrywide problem of selecting a central processing unit (CPU) with response time good enough to satisfy requirements. With a centralized, cluster-type system (whether mainframe- or minicomputer-based) a CPU with more processing power than is needed initially has to be purchased. At a later time, however, the applications environment might outgrow that CPU.

The only option with a cluster solution is to buy bigger and bigger CPUs until the needed power is achieved and even that does not guarantee an acceptable response time. A centralized system presents the constant problem of an uneven loading of resources depending on current usage and unavoidable load fluctuations. Thus it becomes prone to imbalance and consequent reductions in resource utilization.

Of course, a network architecture requires software able to drive the hardware. Thus a key issue in choosing a LAN is the availability of protocols and routines to enable one microprocessor to access another's memory. The most appealing approach is to use several nodes so WS modules can operate asynchronously.

One of the key problems with a LAN architecture concerns the allocation of space on the hard disk while a read or write is going on. The system must be designed to permit the allocation of additional storage space for documents transferred from WS memory. However, if all the storage is filled and space has to be allocated on another disk, several documents could somehow get intertwined. This problem is further compounded by the appearance of static problems due to the office environment. The coaxial cable is a static pathway:

- If a static discharge occurs at one workstation or printer, it may not affect that workstation or printer.
- Instead the discharge can ripple down the cable and affect the file server, another workstation, or the printer.

Both physical and logical solutions are necessary. One manufacturer solved the problem by grounding everything in sight, putting aluminum foil everywhere, and spraying conductive paint on the interior of the WS. Office personnel were warned to be careful in removing the floppy disks in the office environment, where carpets and items of clothing often generate static discharges.

If the floppy was removed and someone walked across the rug with it and touched a piece of metal, an arc could be discharged across the disk and thus destroy all the data on it. Unfortunately, this problem is independent of the equipment being used and occurs often in offices. Electrostatic charge is one of the constraints to be studied carefully prior to implementation.

Logical precautions also are necessary. One thing to be designed into the software is a way to recover almost all the data except the last few keystrokes if the system goes down. This is particularly necessary because most users don't have text and data storage backup systems.

The next most important issue is the applications software. In principle, this should come in packages; and in fact, WP was the first broad applications area in which packages were widely accepted by users. In DP and WP the estimated 5000 packages current in 1984 were growing at 500 percent per year and the 750 companies at 30 percent per year. But packaged software may not meet all needs, particularly in a complex environment. Fourth-generation languages (4GL) are the answer. Computer-based, easy to use and with high productivity, they make feasible a thorough, documented systems analysis necessary to establish user requirements and incorporate add-on functions toward a complete, well-balanced operating environment.

Custom-made approaches are the other alternative. Nearly half of IBM high-end installations surveyed in a recent study reported more than a 2-year backlog of new applications waiting to be implemented. Time and again, the shortage of in-house software staff resources is a serious constraint and the single largest inhibitor to new applications development.

Balancing the application expectations is all the more necessary because with DP/WP integration the resulting environment will range from document handling and data entry to management information systems and the attachment of multiple-use peripherals. The three outstanding features are:

- The WS
- DB management
- Communications

While a LAN may connect a two-digit number of WSs and a three-digit megabyte of memory, it is absolutely essential to foresee interconnection to additional word processing and computer systems in the same office or at other locations. Files created and edited as documents on a given system must be transmitted, automatically stored, and subsequently edited, displayed, or printed.

Human Engineering

If "instant success" has been one of the great myths of our time, another is that computers process most of the text and data required in our offices. Even in the most automated companies, nearly all managers and their secretarial staffs still maintain manual files of statistics pertinent to their daily work, and they can hardly do without them.

Furthermore, one of the major misconceptions of many DP professionals is that all office information can be reduced to bits and bytes. There is surprising failure to realize that office information represents a dynamic interchange of concepts conveyed largely through informal, often fragile, interpersonal communications. It is not simply statistics and texts. Another misconception often encountered is that text, image, and voice can be handled in the same old ways used for data processing in the 1950s. This is the negation of the basic premise behind the merger of data processing and word processing.

The last thing executives and office employees need is some more nonfunctional, nonusable automation of the kind implemented with the first computer generation and later repeated. The workstation that is a repetition of those errors will be the most useless device in the office. Successful office automation requires

- Careful planning
- Applications choices
- Software screening
- Equipment selection
- Human resource management

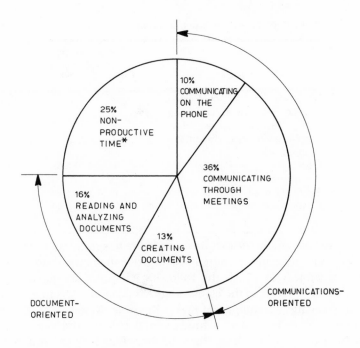

*TRAVELING, FILING, SEARCHING FILES, SEEKING
INFORMATION, TELEPHONE TAG.

FIGURE 7. Management time distribution.

If we say our primary aim is to enhance managerial productivity, we should start by providing ourselves with the needed documentation on what the executive is doing. In one study it was found that a quarter of the executive's time is plainly nonproductive. The statistics are given in Figure 7, and Table 8 details why it is so. The other three-quarters is largely divided between two activities:

- Communicating
- Documenting

Communicating is done through two media. The most time-consuming of the two is meetings; the other is the telephone. Together they account for 46 percent of the executive's time. Another 29 percent is devoted to the handling of documents. The larger part is reading and analyzing received documents; the smaller is creating new documents for other executives to read.

TABLE 8 Executive time allocation

	Portion per day	
Activity	Percent	Hours
Nonproductive: traveling, filing, re-doing previously accomplished tasks such as searching files, seeking information, and telephone tag	25	2.0
Meetings	36	2.88
Telephone	10	.80
Reading and analyzing documents	16	1.28
Creating documents	13	1.04
	100	8.00

Once we have made the diagnosis, the time has come for the prescription. What can office automation do to improve managerial productivity? This is the subject to which the following chapters are devoted. As a preview, Table 9 presents the claims made by a leading OA manufacturer of the time savings its equipment makes possible. Regardless of whether the claims are realistic, it is a fundamental rule in systems work that only with proper studies can there be benefits. Proper studies mean experimentation and documentation:

- To some of us experimentation and documentation are attractive.
- To others they are frustrating.
- But it is unrealistic to hope for results without a fundamental, well-documented applications background.

TABLE 9 Feasible executive time savings through OA

Activity	Percent improvement*	Hours saved per day
Nonproductive	22.5	0.45
Meetings	14.0	0.40
Telephone	24.0	0.19
Reading and analyzing documents	10.0	0.12
Creating documents	17.5	0.18
Improvement per day	16	1.34
Annual total, hours	327.5	
Annual total, weeks	8.2	

* Percent improvement over the times listed in Table 8.

Applications-wise, we must analyze the capabilities, potential benefits, and potential harm of new technical developments. Consider, as an example, the case of electronic funds transfer (EFT) systems. By appreciating the ways in which automated teller machines enable the public to bank, we can develop a new set of services. But also, by studying the ways in which realtime funds-transfer systems may be susceptible to credit blackouts, we should be alerted to the potential harm of haphazard developments.

In any system analysis, since our study should emphasize human factors, we should suspect that a technology that enlarges the information processing capacity of people or organizations by orders of magnitude must have potent influences on their interaction and work techniques. What kinds of differences do computers and communications-based information make in the activities performed by and within organizations? This is a vital subject on which literature is deficient. Most of the accounts of the impact of computing on organizational life focus on

- The ways in which computing alters the notion of organizational effectiveness
- The means by which decisions are made
- The procedures through which activities are structured
- The kinds of control managers can exercise in their administrative domains
- The power of different participants to influence the activities of their departments

In spite of the vital importance of those issues, very little is said about human engineering, including the ways in which the computers and communications-based workstations can alter our lives. The initial training is mainly psychological: The "users to be" must get motivated to live in the new environment while the analysts need both technical competence and moral support.

As Figure 8 demonstrates, there are twelve vital components in an office automation effort; they range from word and data processing to human engineering. Most of these elements are composites of functions: Image and graphics includes facsimile and also video presentation and the visual part of teleconferencing. Audio involves the handling of voice mail, voice synthesis, and voice recognition. And all twelve elements together contribute to decision support and management productivity.

The integrated office services should be studied in Figure 8 perspective. The approach is far removed from the classical DP attitude toward problem solving: people, organizations, and procedures should adapt

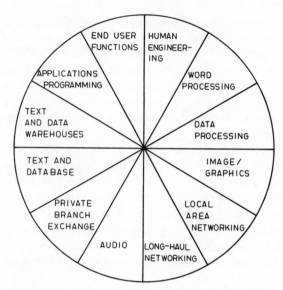

FIGURE 8. There are twelve vital components in an
OA effort; they range from word and data processing
to human engineering.

to DP equipment and techniques. In the past, the latter worked well
despite

- A great deal of user resistance and dissatisfaction with expensive,
  frequently difficult-to-use DP solutions
- The fact that the DP solutions removed control from operating
  management and put it in the hands of data processing management

But useful results can no longer be obtained by sticking to old methods.
That is why human engineering considerations should come first: Relat-
ing the person to the workplace and intensifying that relation as both
the reason for being and the goal of the workstation. Only then come
the mechanics of word, data, and image processing.

Let's recapitulate. Word processing helps to bring the computer
into the office. In doing so, WP is becoming the standard technology
for preparing information in the form of written words—extending beyond the preparation of letters, memos, reports, and other documents.
It is becoming a utility for basic communications from input preparation
to expediting, receiving, and filing, and it thereby provides support to
managers and professionals.

In contrast, data processing helps people handle structured data,
often numerical. This operation is crucial to most organizations, because

numbers are among the key elements in most firms. Historically, centralized and batch data processing, helped by technology, slowly made its way into a distributed frame of reference assisting management and office workers at all levels do their jobs. But DP has also been the test bed for newer disciplines such as the handling of images. The goal of image processing is to present complex data in the form of numbers and words in simple visual forms. As such, image processing includes

- Facsimile
- Display graphics
- Teleconferencing

All three can play an important role in improving productivity: If 100 pages of numerical information can be expressed in a single visual form, not only can great amounts of time be saved in assessing and conveying the meaning of that information but comprehension by others can be greatly enhanced.

By using visual forms, we can add a new perspective to the interpretation of information. Images allow us to see relationships and make connections in the context of time and events; they permit us to show trends and tendencies; they pinpoint deviations and can guide the hand of management in taking corrective action. This broader approach to managerial and clerical services has induced firms to make investments in computer hardware. Exxon, for example, has installed an estimated 1800 minicomputer systems worldwide. To that should be added some 2000 office system terminals—about 20 kinds of them, including Vydec, Wang, and Datapoint.

Office system terminals handle electronic messaging via a corporate message-switching system; Telesystems protocol converters allow Vydecs to talk to Wangs. For a parallel electronic mail service, Exxon uses the Comet service, via Telenet, with fifteen locations served around the globe. This may not be a typical case, but it's a way of corporate life which will increasingly get acceptance. We have to prepare for it from all sides, from the technical level as well as that of human engineering. *The workstation is for the end user.*

Financial and Social Issues

Productivity and profitability are behind the fact that demand for high-speed data communications and videoconferencing is expected to grow 20 to 40 percent annually over the remaining 1980s. By 1990, industry analysts estimate, business will spend $150 billion a year on communications equipment and services—provided the systems pay for themselves.

Payback will come by way of higher productivity—clerical and also, if not particularly, managerial. For instance, in a 5000-person administrative organization, the annual cost for personnel is about $150 million. If automated communications systems can improve productivity 8 percent, the savings to the organization will be $12 million. To achieve that saving, businesses could invest $8000 to $10,000 per employee and recover the cost in 3 years.

Texas Instruments experience, for example, demonstrates how a company can realize substantial savings with an automated information and communications system. Company officials report an 8 percent overall productivity gain. Significantly, a good share of that was realized by the professional and technical workforce. Such statistics have attracted management attention, and they lie behind estimates that capital investment per office worker will rise from about $2000 in 1984 to between $10,000 and $12,000 in 1990. Worldwide expenditures for office automation equipment may reach $80 billion by the turn of the decade.

If that sounds too high, cost reasons can be found for it. Some fairly reliable estimates are that equipment, compensation, and support costs for white-collar workers will reach the $1.5 trillion mark by 1990 in the United States alone. Companies expecting to survive with that level of office costs will be desperate for the productivity gains promised by office automation.

Another statistic reveals the nature of hidden costs. In the early 1980s, surveys were telling us that American business offices dealt with an estimated 325 billion documents. That number grows by 72 billion pieces each year. Though we cannot expect office automation to totally reduce this blizzard of paper that is paralyzing the business office, it is conceivable that a properly planned OA system will be free of heavy dependence on paper-based information.

Remember, however, that machines do not do the work of their own will or on their own initiative. *Problems are never solved by throwing money at them.* Behind every success story is careful preparation, know-how, concrete objectives, and motivation. That's the role human engineering has to play.

Another role closely associated with human engineering is one to be assessed through a fundamental study of social issues. To identify the social impact of computers and communications, we must have, at least implicitly, a theory of the power that OA systems can exert upon individuals, groups, organizations, institutions, social networks, and other human entities. An enlightened approach is to pay proper attention to social information and training. It is hard to believe that the public could best be served by rapid development of a poorly understood technology. Developing the knowhow of computing technologies and their applications is very important, but obtaining public approval is just as vital.

Yet it is disheartening that only a handful of scholars have undertaken serious, well-grounded investigations of the social effects of computer use. Their studies have influenced some aspects of public policy regarding privacy of personal information, but that is only the tip of the iceberg. The pace and scope of new developments in the computer and communications field outstrip the capability of our society to understand the near- and long-term social repercussions.

As of today, there is a common set of beliefs about the influence of computer use on organizational record-keeping systems. Companies (and governmental organizations using computer-based file systems) do collect more personally sensitive data about individuals than other entities do, and they also share data about selected individuals more easily. That eventually leads to serious losses of individual privacy.

We also know, as Raymond Aron* remarked, that a society will not be totally transformed by computers and communications—even though machines and technological factors are an essential factor in social transformation. Center-of-power problems will persist, and with them will come the difficulty for a large part of the population to enter in the "empire of knowledge." (The new empires are those of the mind, Churchill once suggested.)

Financial and social issues, applications perspectives and software, and the evolution of the workplace itself provide plain evidence that technology is much greater than the physical device. The package includes:

- Hardware and software facilities
- Diverse set of skills
- Organizational units to supply and maintain computer-based text and data
- Sets of beliefs about what is good for what and how it may influence management action and the social structure at large

Difficulties that users face in exploiting computers and communications lie in the way the overall package is embedded in a complex set of social relationships. This is brought into sharper perspective by the way OA systems reach the workplace online and are effectively shared with other users. The OA systems often depend on text and data that are provided through several different social networks and which entail

---

* The late Raymond Aron was the patriarch of French reporters and political commentators.

contact with different organizational groups. The user's involvement with a given OA system occurs at a point along a career trajectory. When an online system is embedded in a complex social setting, it becomes a social object and its usage becomes a social act.

Inevitably, social issues play a vital role in the sense of acceptance. *Most users of information systems don't know a bit from a byte and could not care less. But they do care about the aftermaths:* As every management knows, success in a pioneering effort can be emotionally and psychologically rewarding—whereas failure leads to social and financial distress.

Technical Notes

Bandwidth, narrow band, baseband, wide band, and *broadband* have to do with the wave frequencies on which all forms of telephony, radio, TV, and microwave transmissions depend. Some portions of the available range of frequencies are best suited to one or the other kind of transmission or transmission content; they are the *bands.* "Wide," or "broad," bands have aptly been defined as more channel capacity than we need at this time. The layman need not be concerned with the details.

The *cursor* is a bright rectangle on the screen manipulated by the user through the keyboard or a mouse. It marks a position directly related to a location in the screen and serves as a pointer. The cursor is also positioned through software. When, for example, text is being entered by typing it on the keyboard, the cursor moves ahead and marks the spot where the next character will be formed. In the event of an error of, say, an x for an s, the cursor can be moved over the misstrike and the correct letter typed in. At the same time it appears on the screen, the character is entered in memory.

Moving the cursor requires manipulating keys marked with arrows for up and down and for left and right, which can be a slow process. An alternative is the *mouse,* which when moved about on a horizontal surface causes the cursor to move also. The cursor is still positioned by eye and hand, but the mouse process is both faster and more comfortable than using keys. Also, the mouse lets the user exercise any one of several options to modify material displayed on the screen and marked by the cursor. (See Figure 25.) Other means of avoiding input by keyboard are the *light pen, touch-sensitive screen,* and *graphic tablet.*

The *central processing unit* is roughly comparable to the engine in an automobile: It does what the program determines that the machine should do.

CHAPTER 5

Productivity Goals

Seven-eighths of anything can't be seen.

GEORGE MARSHALL

Studies have indicated that 5 billion pieces of paper are generated annually and that this number doubles every few years. The cost of federal paperwork alone is $100 billion per year, and it increases with each new set of laws passed by Congress. All this paperwork is generated, maintained, stored, and retrieved by a method that has seen only minimal change in the last century: each document has been typed—manually.

The situation is getting worse, and that statement is just as valid whether we talk of American or European business. In a study in Italy IBM found that in one year its typical branch office had in archives 20,600 pages with 5.5 million words. These were subsequently divided by origin: 79 percent from other IBM offices and 21 percent from external entities.

In Holland, statistics derived from an office automation study demonstrate that *only* the thirty-second of the files being examined is the *right one*. The balance are irrelevant to the case under examination; they are retrieved (and then stored again) because of false identification.

It should, therefore, come as no surprise that banks, insurance, manufacturing, marketing, and other industries have had a keen interest in revamping the workstation: turning it inside out, eliminating the floating paper, putting it online, and, in the process, improving the productivity of the clerical personnel. These are very worthwhile goals provided the most important issue—managerial productivity—is given the attention it deserves.

Online storage and retrieval of text and data has raised the question of interactive versus batch solutions, with some companies being ahead of others in this respect. IBM in Santa Teresa (the brain factory) employs one terminal per person in its service, but 0.1 terminal per person is allocated to test areas, conference rooms, and the like. The 2200 online terminals so employed are mainly personal computers.

That example, and many others like it, point to interactive environments. The interactive environments are coming, but let's not forget what experience so often documents: It takes much more than putting a machine at a workplace to increase employee productivity. That is a principle I never tire of stating, because I find that it is so often misunderstood. Parts 2 and 3 of this book are dedicated to it.

Costs of Clerical Productivity

For a long stretch of years—from the end of the Second World War to the early 1970s—productivity showed significant gains. Then, suddenly, it slowed down; it reached its peak in 1978, and it has been falling since. Meanwhile, office labor costs have doubled.

- Studies indicate that clerical and secretarial workers are no more than 40 to 60 percent as productive as they could be.

- Executive productivity is thought to be only 60 to 75 percent of what it might be.

Such statistics are characteristic of the United States and western Europe. Yet we must also appreciate that assessing office productivity is fairly difficult. How do we measure the productivity of a secretary? Of an administrative assistant? By the number of words typed? By telephone calls made? How do we assess the value of employee morale to a business? The total productivity of the organization? The effectiveness of management?

The more complex these questions are, the deeper we must look into the fundamentals, the more we must be sure that the prerequisites are in place. It is hardly a question of distributing the tools. In a strictly technical sense, most of the pieces of the office of the future are here, but we are still far from the fully integrated, cost-justified, flexible, powerful set of systems that we know we need to improve office productivity.

Continued technological change, cost trends, user tailoring, training requirements, current incompatibilities, and a great many other factors inhibit the rational utilization of the available resources. Perhaps the greatest inhibition comes from not knowing how to best use the machines we have developed.

One of the areas in which knowhow is thinnest is that of assuring a nominal evolution in office systems: both protecting the daily flow of procedures needed to run the business and providing the ground for the gradual change to the new environment. Hence, there is a crying need for a 5-year plan to help provide for transition.

Costs are another handicap. Current expenses run way ahead because of inflation, and that leaves the company short of the budget necessary for the change. Inflation is confounding attempts by management to contain costs. The price of the office's raw material, paper, rose 110 percent between 1973 and 1980. As the mass of paper further expands, costs are pushed higher and productivity declines. One estimate is that there are, on average, eight file drawers of information containing some 18,000 documents for every white-collar worker in America. Together, the country's white-collar workers produce 72 billion documents annually and maintain and file another 300 billion or so. The information explosion seems to be proceeding at a rate of about two file drawers per office worker each year, and the end is not in sight.

These statistics on the glut of paper and the associated high costs help explain why half-baked measures and machine-by-machine replacements cannot do the job. What is necessary is a system able to handle management communications and support integrated voice, text, data, and image. Such a system can provide rapid information access and distribution, reduce paper flow, and greatly increase the productivity of the office professional and clerical staff.

In any effort to reduce paper flow, it should never be lost from sight that years of ill-conceived practice have made paperwork a very big activity in most companies. That is a basic reason why the goal of replacing anything like 90 percent of the paper with computers and communications in the span of a 5-year program would be a challenging one. The company must not only realign executive responsibilities for meeting this objective but also enlist employee participation and support. Because paper has its disciples throughout the organization, a sensitive approach is to announce a policy of gradually reducing the flow of paper, with the ultimate aim of abolishing it. No "great leap forward" should be contemplated—it would fall flat.

The 5-year plan finds its best justification in these terms: It takes at least 3 to 5 years for any reasonably complex new idea to spread fairly widely through the organization. The acceptance and use of new ideas follows an ogive curve: a slow start followed by acceleration when opinion leaders adopt the innovation.

The effort toward innovation should be both internal (affecting the systems and procedures of the firm) and external (toward clients, suppliers, and regulatory agencies). Citibank, for example, sought to improve customer services while holding the line on rising text and data processing costs. A basic step in this strategy was the provision of an effective solution to the problem of office productivity: using computer technology to help managers and professionals work more effectively.

In the mid-1970s, Citibank had 50,000 employees and a 6-to-1 span-of-control ratio which involved slightly over 8000 managers. If computer technology could be employed to improve the span of control by, say, 12 percent, 1000 fewer managers would be needed and savings to the bank would amount to nearly $50 million per year.*

The longer-term strategic consideration led, in 1976, to a study that covered the activities of some 150 managers in three divisions. The work these managers were doing was carefully recorded to document how they spent their time. Statistics indicated that professionals spend about 3 hours a day communicating.

If workstations can improve overall efficiency (including communications) by 10 percent, an impressive number of workhours per day can be saved, and there are about 280 workdays per year. But if managers are to access information whenever they want it, communicate effectively with their peers, and make more informed, faster decisions, then they need a totally integrated and user-friendly system. It should combine functions, like word processing, communications, and data processing, previously available only individually. A single workstation must handle text manipulation for clerical staff and communications and tracking functions for management. Beyond that, satisfying a user's productivity needs is one thing but satisfying the individual worker's needs and accommodating that worker's skills is another.

Ease of use is of major importance in all processing functions; a system that's easy to learn and operate is absolutely essential. Components must be designed with the user in mind and engineered to minimize operator fatigue and eyestrain. Simplicity of use is a bonus.

Another factor that must be considered is people's reluctance to work with high-technology equipment. To the end user, the presentation of information can be much more important than information content. That is one of the basic characteristics of interactive approaches, and it contrasts sharply with batch processing. In the latter the format and quality of the output are secondary in importance to the information contained in it.

However, success can be elusive if the total effort is not backed

---

* In fact, that is precisely what has taken place. Because of its advanced degree of automation and able employment of technology, Citibank reached a 7-to-1 span of control in 1984. The next target is 8 to 1.

up with a firm commitment and capability to serve and support a broad user base. That is true also if we fail to look at cost as a significant factor. Unit cost and the economies of mass are intimately linked when we talk of new technologies. A recent study suggested that, to achieve acceptance to a significant order of magnitude, the target purchase price should stand at about $2000 per workstation. To help get the cost down, some functions might be supplied centrally via a company's data communications network, others be provided regionally, and still others be distributed at the workstation level.

But even if workstations are relatively inexpensive—say at the target price of $2000—the pressure should be on making job and organizational changes such that the new systems will be used most efficiently. The distributed workstation needs no sophisticated multiprogramming operating system with the resource management functions we find in a large mainframe. What it does need are a user-friendly interface, interactive features, communications capabilities, and cost per contact hour well below that of a human assistant.

Particular attention should be paid to the goal of avoiding disruptive effects on the technological organization. The potential turbulence from new technological developments can be great, and careful planning of efforts is needed to avoid the negative fallouts. Careful observations on the coming impact of a new system can help in the subsequent implementation of the change.

The wisdom of the 5-year plan I so strongly recommend lies in the above observations. Most companies cannot absorb great changes in a short period of time; they have to spread the changes out. They can do that successfully only when the plan specifies the goals, the resources, and the milestones against which progress toward goal achievement can be measured.

Helping Mental Productivity

It is a known but not always appreciated fact that professionals have not adapted to change as rapidly as they should. When it comes to office automation, the executives themselves usually refer to word processing, and in doing so they miss the whole point. What they really should talk about is management and professional productivity, but many business executives would rather automate anywhere but at their desks.

The hardest part of office automation is overcoming the behavioral problem. The top issues are people, people, and people. And while the focus on automation in the past has been on the support staff, the effort should really be made at the managerial and professional levels;

that is where user benefits are to be realized from improvement in productivity.

We should focus more attention on the executive suite and less on the secretary's desk. We must study how managers and other professionals waste their time in the office. IBM estimates that there are nine *principals* (office employees who can delegate work) for every secretary. And when salaries and fringe benefits are taken into account, the ratio of costs is roughly 30 to 1 rather than 9 to 1.

Executives and white-collar professionals account for about three-fourths of total office costs. Also, relative to what they are hired to do, managers are actually far less productive than most of them assume they are. As a recent study helps document, "knowledge workers"

- Spend remarkably little time—less than 30 percent of the week—performing actual *thought* work
- Spend a disproportionate amount, 45 percent, in meetings
- Spend the other 25 percent in diverse and unproductive activities such as telephone tag, in which the parties call each other many times a day but never speak until sometime tomorrow

Better organization, including prepared agendas, agreed-upon discipline, interactive terminals, and orderly access to databases, can halve such time-consuming tasks. A well-advised serious study will start with audio mail to eliminate telephone tag. Next should come the provision of interactive capabilities for query purposes, then data and text handling (basically word processing and dictation), and finally electronic mail. In greater detail, the executive services should involve (Figure 9) the following:

1. **Calendar Services.** The workstation should have a computer-supported calendar facility. Time periods must be displayed: the current week, the next month, and the next three months. Further-out periods are presented with successively less detail. For instance, the next month and the next three months can be used for blocking out time for trips, important meetings, vacations, setting appointments, and rearranging meetings to agree with executive needs and availabilities.

The user of such calendar services can maintain a personal calendar, allocate appointments and free time, and review the calendar at a glance by day, week, or month. Though users cannot see each other's calendars, they can ask the system to arrange appointments with other users or groups of users by specifying desired dates and times. An appointment is formally scheduled only when all parties confirm the schedule.

A computer-based calendar system can effectively assist the executive

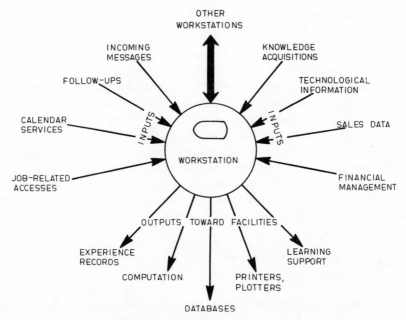

FIGURE 9. Range of facilities which should be supported by an executive workstation.

by keeping track of all appointments, automating name and address lists for all correspondence and memos, accessing company reports in the data processing files, and making sure that schedule variations will be brought to the attention of the responsible executive as programmed.

2. **Personal Files.** Through closed user group (CUG) services, users can set up files accessible only by themselves or by a limited number of other persons. This opens up interactive systems to a wide variety of uses with important consequences in the substitution of online database access for paper.

When it comes to personal files, there are a multitude of possibilities to be implemented; they have to do both with what is stored in the infopages and with the routing (index page) capabilities. Examples are direct addressing, simplified menu options, workstation level display of text as it will appear when printed, and a semigraphics option that allows word wrap-around within an organizational chart type of display.

3. **Voice Mail.** Store-and-forward voice-switching services will grow rapidly in popularity in the late 1980s. The underlying trend in traffic may be away from voice and toward more structured types of message communications; but voice messages are still the easiest form of

implementation, and they will retain a good share of future communications capabilities.

Incoming telephone messages can be placed directly into the private branch exchange (PBX) of the office automation system. They can be assigned an action, whether to file, to be commented on, or to be redirected to another individual for response. There is also a reminder function, which automatically notifies the recipient on a given day that a certain task is to be performed or action taken.

Voice mail services that were in development at the time of writing will provide national mailbox capabilities for businessmen on the road. Distribution of voice messages will complement the electronic services handling documents. They could include direct transmission to a PBX at a subscriber's office or a next-day mailgram-type delivery to that or another location.

4. **Decision Support Systems.** The managerial workstation will increasingly incorporate decision support capabilities including the use of routines for analyzing data, forecasting, testing what-if conditions, and generally enlarging the planning and control capabilities of the executive.

Decision support features will help professional people manage their time more effectively. But their implementation involves interfacing with management to determine requirements, design the product, and later modify it as management's needs change and technology permits further perfecting of decision support tools.

5. **Electronic Mail (Teletex).** The object of electronic mail is to enable managers and professionals to send and receive documents to and from each other or multiple users on a distribution list. All documents, whether they are text, data, notes, or memos, are secure from unauthorized access because a user must have an identification code and password to handle documents in this system.

Among the facilities now supported by teletex systems are full note and memo creation capabilities; distribution, forward, or redistribution of documents and notes; annotations of received messages; delivery times specified by the user; receipt of acknowledgements; and the implementation of security codes.

Workstation systems can include the capability to communicate with other workstations by way of the telephone network. Supporting facilities are electronic mail, voice mail, calendaring, expert systems, correspondence management, and the report preparation and retrieval discussed later in this chapter.

6. Electronic In-Basket.   A computer and communications system can effectively maintain an electronic in-basket for its executive user. The in-basket receives and stores notes, documents, and appointment requests until some action is taken on them. The user can read, file, annotate, and redistribute anything in or delete anything from the in-basket.

The system typically notifies the user that something is in the in-basket by flashing the word "in-basket" on the user's workstation. Depending on the sophistication of the software, the in-basket can store and index, as in a personal Rolodex file, and thereby allow the user to develop a database management application without knowing anything about databases. The same package can support an intrasite electronic message system.

7. Report Preparation.   With a distributed information system, each major activity within an organization can obtain computer support for the production of report data on its activities. Any executive can use the workstation to pull together report data for all areas under his or her responsibility and prepare the required management memos and reports.

Executives can use their workstations to access authorized databases and retrieve financial and technical report data for the activities that fall within their responsibilities. Any workstation user can access both inside and outside databases in this manner, subject to authorization privileges.

8. Correspondence Management.   Correspondence management is a logical extension of the above-mentioned capabilities; it offers document storage and retrieval capabilities that aid in paper reduction and facilitate filing. Documents can be filed by using any of several filing codes, as well as title, author, category, document number, and date created.

Once filed, the document can be retrieved by using any of the keys used in filing, which allows the user to view it as if multiple copies had been filed: Only one copy of the document may actually be on the system at any one time, but it can be retrieved as if multiple copies existed.

Filing Premises

Reasonably sophisticated software permits users to establish filing codes on a per-document basis, allows documents to be deleted, eases archiving and restoring, facilitates inquiries of all sorts, and produces a total service support which far exceeds past capabilities of processing transactions on a computer.

These capabilities can be exercised in the broad area of management communications. They make it feasible for executives not only to send and distribute documents and messages of any size electronically, but they also provide additional features such as the ability to annotate a received document or letter before filing or forwarding it. Document security and access are controlled by the originator. The cost savings made possible by these structured approaches can hardly escape top management's attention in view of AT&T's having been forced to raise telephone rates by 160 percent between 1970 and 1977. There were further significant increases of local telephone rates after the AT&T divestiture, although competition saw to it that long-distance rates dropped.

That electronic message systems can make a major contribution to cost control becomes evident when we consider that office workers in the United States currently make about 100 billion telephone calls a year at an average cost of 15 cents per call. That adds up to $15 billion a year. Furthermore, the average manager spends 80 percent of his time just in transmitting or receiving information—though not all of it by telephone.

The message to be read in those statistics is that, at the managerial level of implementation, multifunction workstations are basic to office automation; the equipment is intended for use by managers and professionals. Many units have been specifically designed for the markets they are to serve. But we need to plan carefully for them in order to avoid the types of major mistakes that were made, for example, when computers and word processing systems were first installed.

A carefully planned network is necessary both to assure performance and· to contain the costs. Multifunction workstations may well end up representing the major capital investment for office automation and distributed information systems because of their potentially large numbers. Because of the multiple functionality, the microprocessor support, and the storage capabilities, workstations will eventually replace the telephone, in- and out-baskets, file cabinets, memo pads, copiers, and calculators—in short, much of what is found in the typical executive's work area.

In the applications area under consideration, the user is assumed to be intelligent but not skilled in man-machine interactions. Thus he or she should be guided into correct actions and politely guided away from incorrect ones but never made to feel abandoned, lost, or disliked. That puts a heavy burden on the designer of the user-friendly interfaces—and the analyst who must father the system to its maturity. And though neither is the technology perfectly ready nor is the economics totally clear, we should start now to prepare for the day when the integrated solution to office automation will be practical and economically justifiable.

The approach described above will alter in a significant way our way of looking at the administrative duties. Traditionally, with the advent of the formal organizational structure, the main function of the administrative office has been support of management decision making. Equipment installed to assist in that process has to be rich in communications methods, which are fundamental to increasing efficiency and aggregate productivity throughout the organization.

But all the methodologies to which we have been accustomed support the illusion that administrative activities are relatively simple and easily standardized, the patterns and contents of transactions are relatively stable, and procedural relationships are well established and that there is a fairly simple system for analyzing the cost and value of service. Those are the prerequisites for non-computer-based decision making, but industrial and financial life suggests that they are not often met. In real life we must understand the complex trade-offs between various alternatives for achieving adequate performance in decision making.

By increasing the size of the clerical staff, we further handicap clear decision making. When additional clerical and administrative labor is hired to deal with the errors, inconsistencies, and exceptional cases generated by the operating system, the number of special conditions and unresolved cases increases rather than shrinks. Far from producing economies of scale, large staffs tend to increase the complexity and cost of what used to be a simple process.

Making procedural changes in a complex administrative network is especially difficult. Interdepartmental relationships reflect the relative clout enjoyed by each component, one that is directly translatable into status, authority, and precedence in decision making. Furthermore, when structural relationships in an organization are upset, a large share of the total time of knowledge workers is occupied by the process of managing procedural changes as missions are adjusted. These are some of the fundamental reasons why computers and communications can put the classical process of decision support in a new perspective.

Building the Right Productivity Image

When our images are unrealistic, our decisions will inevitably lead to disappointment. Therefore, we must gain more accurate images of the future from which to choose and subsequently develop better ways to reevaluate them. This is a steady process.

Images of the future are formed by projecting patterns that we perceive in the records of the past. Hence, improving our view of the future involves better handling of the records of the past. We must perceive patterns in the records which we think will be repeated. Such patterns may be of three main types:

1. The better known are mechanical, stable patterns. They consist essentially of the stable behavior which is characteristic of deterministic models.

Billing, accounts receivable, and accounts payable are examples; they parallel the mathematical models that make it possible to predict eclipses and other solar system phenomena.

2. Less known, but still manageable, is time series.

Here the behavior is probabilistic but the laws behind the processes being investigated follow a given pattern. Sales forecasts, inventory management, and other optimization and allocation procedures are examples.

Macroscopic examples are broader and more complex applications of time series. Economic cycles, inflation, depressions, and wars have a certain repetitive (episodic) character which we attempt to study through mathematical models.

Often the fine distinction between mechanical, deterministic models and stochastic, probabilistic models is obscured through the lack of clear understanding of the forces involved. The search for mechanical patterns in random series can only lead to superstition—the perception of order where there is none.

3. Fairly well known are stochastic situations in which a large number of parameters interact with one another.

This is the general pattern of change and evolution. It is much less predictable than the pattern of single episodes, because it contains many such episodes.

If, for example, we postulate an equilibrium of the international economy (or of an ecological system), the interactions are too complex to support a clear prediction of the path toward the equilibrium—and the nature of the movements which are involved. The number of parameters in biological ecosystems is very large; the number in economic and social systems is even larger. We are constantly being surprised by parameters that we have failed to identify—and by relationships we have not been able to predict.

Nobody predicted the social aftermaths of the Industrial Revolution. Nobody predicted the automobile and its effects. Nobody predicted the computer. And nobody is seriously venturing into a prediction of the social aftermaths of the knowledge revolution. Yet, it is hard to believe that our perception of the world cannot be significantly improved, and with it our image of the future.

We can conclude this discussion by repeating the key issues to which reference has been made. The new management support devices will, to a large measure, derive from computer-based interactivity between the end user and the information stored in the database. Direct, online man-information communication is the best answer that current technology can give to the question of how to get higher productivity in the management of industrial economies.

Computers and communications equipment can transform office work. The capability exists, but advantage of it is not being taken. On the contrary, it is being resisted. Three reasons can be pinpointed: people are frightened by video screens; managers do not know which equipment to choose; and the methodology for measuring productivity is not yet ready.

The problem of finding a way through that resistance is urgent, because there seems to be a causal link between developments in the information sector and improving productivity. Since office workers have been sluggish in improving productivity (but not in getting higher wages) the shift to an information-based economy might be inherently inflationary. Yet "doing something" means reducing resistance to innovation, and that resistance is quite strong.

Adoption of the new technologies will be eased through adequate demonstration of possible benefits. For instance, a director of finance equipped with the personal workstation that we propose could monitor budget, taxation, investment, and other information needs, and thereby obtain comprehensive insight into the financial condition of the firm over a broad range of services.

The personal workstation would become the single most important extension of training and experience. When augmented by a system providing authorization, password, security, validation, and history review capabilities, the financial executive could deliver services now available only through central offices burdened with extensive bureaucracy and long response times.

Typically, the personal workstation will support at the local level comprehensive and easy-to-implement end user functions (EUF), while compunications (the merger of computers and communications) will make it feasible to access text, data, image, and voice mail stored in distributed databases (DDB). The local functions, the line, and the access mechanisms will incorporate a significant amount of intelligence based on microprocessors. This network of EUF and DDB is the best tool that technology now puts at our disposal to minimize the proliferation of information related to increasing organizational complexity. When properly implemented, it can assure that all parties will examine facts from a common base, which is clearly helpful when operational procedures are to be adjusted.

"Properly implemented" means avoiding the wasteful information management that is common when organizations have neither the means for measuring the costs of processing transactions (or accessing databases for management queries) nor the means of assessing the value of services delivered to users. Transaction costs are better understood when information services are delivered as a product (for instance, the current balance of a bank account) because commercial viability is affected by the ability to manage such requests. The lines are not as clear, however, when we talk of administrative services—unless specific goals are set up in advance.

Hence, we will be well advised to take our lessons from the organizations which have begun accumulating valid experience. A management information system, such experience demonstrates, does better when it delivers service to managers who trust it most, delivers quality, and delivers promptly. Generally it gains the confidence of the people it serves.

Reaching the Productivity Goal

Access to databases and efficient communications links are the pillars on which management productivity rests. High technology helps structure both of them if we know how to do our duty and are dedicated to using our skills.

Distributed information services make feasible a whole new way of looking at databases. If the company's vital information is stored in a distributed manner, is properly classified and identified, is supported by data dictionaries, and is made available interactively to the end user, all kinds of possibilities arise for inserting computers and communications into management's decision-making process.

Rebuilding the communications aspects of an operating industrial organization or financial institution is difficult. Developing new skills without impeding performance is not always easy. Applying the new information technologies are not skills that one can learn overnight, but the skills are vital to conduct of business.

We often fail to recognize how close the merger of formerly diverse facilities is to being realized. Yet the results obtained from innovative applications help show us the future. Consider the experiment on computers and communications by Owens-Corning Fiberglass.

In the late 1970s, like most industrial concerns and financial institutions, Owens-Corning Fiberglass faced significant intracompany communications problems. In late 1978, those problems led to the establishment of a pilot Infoplex electronic mail service. The selected user team was a representative sample of the ultimate user population in the firm (50 percent professionals and related staffs, 35 percent executives, 15 percent clerical), and the results have been positive:

- Three out of four participants reported that Infoplex had a positive influence on their ability to do their work.
- No user reported a negative aftermath or adverse effect.
- The rate of acceptance was directly proportional to the provision of proper user training and "on call" support.

The cost of the service averaged $65 per month per user, but benefit exceeded cost by a significant margin. More precisely, service cost reached $1.18 per message including terminal facilities. But because 72 percent of all telephone calls are unsuccessful on the first try, the company saved 25 cents on every call over traditional methods. Note that two birds are killed with one well-placed stone: First are the cost savings—a matter of great concern to any enterprise in these lean and turbulent times. Second, and most important, is the substitution of electronic mail service for unsuccessful telephone calls.

At Owens-Corning the Infoplex experience was that an average of between four and six daily messages per employee replaced an equal number of telephone calls and their retry factor. Considering a projected user population of 1500 persons, management calculated *replacement savings of $600,000 per year*. These are the projected yearly savings on *physical productivity*.

More significantly, management examined the improvement in employee communications efficiency by evaluating *time saved* over traditional approaches. The analysis demonstrated a dramatic saving of $4.35 per teletex message, which means $900,000 per month or *$10 million per year*. Here we are talking of improvement of *mental productivity*, which exceeds by a factor of 18 that of the physical productivity.

A key factor in reaching such positive results is, of course, ease of use. In all applications of modern technology we should look toward the employment of *friendly* terminals. "Friendly" means simply that the terminals are relatively easy and comfortable to use and that their features are designed with the needs of their operators in mind. Design should facilitate the interfacing of man and machine. "Friendly" also means "informative" and "forgiving."

From these developments derives a whole new strategy: a comprehensive, interactive view of decision support capabilities, the development of new products and services, the application of knowledge toward reaching those goals, and using consulting services as necessary to bring together the facilities for meeting the requirements. Mental productivity particularly stands to benefit.

PART 2

How High Technology Affects Management Practice

CHAPTER 6

Management Looks at Information Systems

Power goes naturally to the factor which is harder to get or replace.

MANAGEMENT PRINCIPLE

Banks, merchandising firms, and industrial companies find themselves today at a crossroads. The challenges are more than anyone might wish to have at the same time, yet they have to be faced. What they have in common is the need for information. As competition tightens and the business pace accelerates, the need for interactive access to databases increases. The databases must be well organized, regularly pruned, and properly dated; they must reflect the real information requirements of the enterprise.

The personal, intelligent workstation (WS) should be the pivot point around which we construct management, office, and factory services. This workstation is a terminal on the desktop or in a desk drawer of the end user. Microprocessor technology has had tremendous effects on the design of the workplace. The microprocessor-based WS is far more potent than the typical computer terminal, and a properly selected baseband microcomputer connection is available at a cost much lower than that of the usual long-haul communications. Typically, such baseband local area networks (LANs) will be linked through a broadband system on an office building, factory, campus, or metropolitan area network.

The very first spreadsheet to be offered as a commodity (Visicalc) made us realize what personal computers stand for; and as we move toward LANs and office automation (OA), we see that the potential in this market is even greater than in the computer field developed so far. It touches every managerial and secretarial desk in business and industry. The cost of a low-end personal computer is now approaching that of an electric typewriter.

Having the situation under instant control through flashes, tables, documents, and graphics displayed on a color terminal would have been only the dream of managers just a few years ago. Today it is a reality.

Microcomputers have given information systems human dimensions, and they have put the man-to-computer relation in new perspective. Today, productivity-type implementations in banking, industry, and business applications represent an estimated 75 percent of the personal computer (PC) market for machines costing more than $1000. And let's always remember that wages and benefits account for some two-thirds of all business costs.

The hardware (HW)—the mechanical, electrical, and electronic gear behind the information system—has become less important than it once was. What is vital is the proper definition of the applications environment and the logical understructure (software, SW) supporting it. The same thing is true of the end user functions (EUF).

An integral part of this whole picture is the problem of managing people, of keeping them on the learning curve. This is just as true of the end users as it is of the system specialists.

- On the users' side, it's a tremendous upheaval for people to get accustomed to the new organization–information system processes which alter even the way of looking at the workplace.

- On the systems specialists' side, it is easy to get comfortable with past practices and hard to shake off bad habits.

Furthermore, many data processing organizations have become overstaffed, self-perpetuating bureaucracies. When overstaffing continues for too long, the risk is dual: underutilizing personnel and losing productivity. Local area networks of personal computers can be instrumental in reversing the productivity curve.

The need for thorough preparation is emphasized by the fact that poorly managed new technology can actually lower productivity. And it is abundantly evident that we should strive for efficiency in personnel utilization and for steady productivity improvement when wages and benefits account for some two-thirds of all business costs.

he Top-Management Meeting

ie product to which this chapter is addressed is the information system
'), the basic goal of which is communications for supporting manage-
nt decisions. This product is for the end user. That approach is new;
mposes a different perspective than the one in which computers,
ommunications, and terminals were viewed for years. It also calls for
a new type of specialist—not a programmer, but one who organizes
and presents information to the person for whom the IS is intended.

These end user information specialists, or whatever we end up calling
them, will be oriented toward business rather than technology. This is
just another manifestation of the way all data processing is changing:
from software and hardware to design, development, implementation,
and maintenance. That was the sense of the discussion which was held
at the top-management level of two leading banks. One had already
implemented a new information system design philosophy based on
personal computers at the workstation level connected to each other
and to a local database through LANs. The other was seeking information
on the experience: Were the results worthwhile? Were they better than
with centralized processing or distributed minis?

Both answers were positive, and for good reasons:

- First, the results were excellent because, for the first time, computer power had reached the executive desk itself.

- Second, how good or bad the solution turned out to be was relative. To a large measure it depended on the validity of the preceding IS solution, the one the organization had applied until then.

The financial institution that had switched to PCs and LANs had
for a decade and a half been a leader in applications online to mainframe.
Yet management had reason to be unhappy. As the senior vice president
of the bank remarked: "My predecessor said: 'There is a fabulous mainframe made for you. Everything is automated!' But reality wasn't so
exciting!" With the online-to-mainframe solution, the treasury and Forex
operation had 28 dumb terminals—and they were not used. Why not?
Because, as the senior vice president explained, they were too difficult
to use and they were not flexible. The Forex (foreign exchange) dealer
for whom they were intended couldn't spend time on a terminal and
let the client on the telephone wait. His first and primary job was to
close the deal.

Since the way in which the application was implemented was not
really good enough, the senior vice president asked for changes in the
computer programs. "Fine," said the data processing (DP) manager,

"but given the backlog in demands, you must wait for 6 months. You must also pay $300,000 for the requested changes."

That caused a reaction: "How can we stop being the slaves of the computer?" A second question was: "How can we evaluate the efficiency of a DP center?" Having asked himself those questions, the senior vice president took them to the bank's policy committee, and practically every member of it had a similar reaction: "So many million dollars are spent every year on computers. Are they spent well or badly?"

But although the members of the executive committee were worried about computer expenditures and usage, they lacked specific IS knowhow to choose an alternative. The central DP bureaucracy offered nothing new, and so change was delayed until some new ideas turned up. They came at a top-management seminar when a professor at MIT said, "The answer to management requirements can no longer be found in mainframes. It lies in personal computers." And he produced an Apple machine.

This made a lasting impression on the senior vice president. Back at his office, he found one of his people who understood the Apple microcomputer and asked him if he wanted to work on this idea. His colleague was indeed interested, and that's how the whole project got started.

Now let's recapitulate, because the lessons of what turned out to be a very successful project are valuable. User needs evolve and therefore both the marketplace and the industry change. *Customers require systems solutions to their information management problems, and they want the computer assistance to be timely and at their desks.*

Changes are necessary. Some of these changes are structural; others are related to technology; still others are related to intensifying competition. Executives need ways to manage a complex environment. The faster the world moves the more they see themselves obliged to store, manipulate, and move the vast quantities of information vital to their particular businesses. Eventually this becomes synonymous with automating their offices for greater productivity.

Mainframes can no longer fill the bill, nor can minis. Traditionally, mainframes have been two degrees remote from the end user (Figure 10), batch-oriented, slow in moving data around, and error-prone. Too many human linkages have contributed to the last shortcoming; they are the weakest links in the chain. Therefore, remote batch operation and movement toward realtime and timesharing by the addition of online terminals did not improve the score. If anything, the "advances" highlighted the pitfalls, the delays, and the uncertainty of the system.

Minicomputers improved the situation somewhat, but the gap between the end user and the information machine remained. With minis

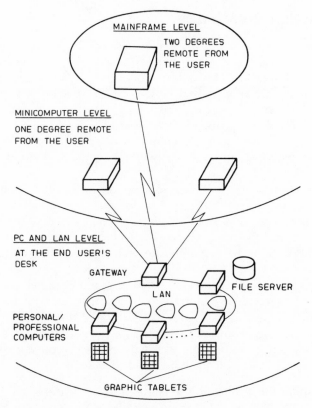

FIGURE 10. Traditionally, mainframes have been two degrees remote from the end user.

the two-degree remoteness of the end user from the information re-source was reduced to one degree. The connection distance, the distance at which terminals could be placed without a communications discipline, increased by nearly an order of magnitude (Table 10). But that did not attack the main problem: the need for effective communications between the user and the information stored in the machine.

TABLE 10   Connection distances

Hardware	Connection distance
Mainframe peripherals	Less than 3 meters
Terminals for mini-based and cluster	Less than 30 meters
PC with baseband LAN	From 330 to 1330 meters
PC with broadband LAN (CATV)	Up to 10 kilometers

93

Establishing a New Policy

To continue with the story, the senior vice president, on returning to his office in London, was determined to attack the problem in the way recommended at MIT. He looked around for a Forex operator who was knowledgeable of personal computers. The man who presented himself was working in sterling-dollar deals. Together he and the vice president defined the problem simply but effectively. Over a weekend a dealer programmed an Apple computer to answer the problems and on Monday morning he could demonstrate that the system was able to do the job.

"I was enthusiastic with the solution, and I said 'let's buy more Apple microcomputers',"* the senior vice president recalls. But as the machines proliferated in number, the need to take a systems look at hard- and software became evident. Particularly important was the need for the workstations to communicate with one another and with the database.

Systems skill was sought after. A young and dynamic information scientist, unburdened by mainframe convictions, was available to work on the project. After a brief study, he suggested that the best solution was to put the microcomputers online in a network and emulate a big computer by implementing an attached resources concept. This preserved the basic system acquisitions made so far by:

1. Developing the application in cooperation with the user
2. Putting it on the desk top
3. Keeping it flexible and simple

Other advantages were:

4. Eliminating the cumbersome, error-prone manual input
5. Canceling the online connections to mainframe and mini
6. Giving the end user the needed power
7. Making available add-on services that were never before possible

Although together those advantages were responsible for project success, management was quick to note that—in retrospect—the most important of all was making the user coresponsible for system development. For the first time, through PC and LAN implementation, the user had found the way to satisfy his or her interests.

---

* This was the first implementation. Since then the operation has been converted to IBM and DEC personal computers.

As the users themselves reported, the flexibility has been tremendous. Management too liked the results: "I did not have to wait 6 months and spend $300,000 for patching," said the senior vice president. "I had the results there and then." A major advantage in operations is reliability. If an IBM PC is down, the end user can roll out the defective machine and roll in a spare. If the mainframe is down, there is a complete halt in the online operations.

Since senior management repeatedly expressed its satisfaction with the PC and LAN solution, one of the participants in a discussion of the project asked about the disadvantages. "They are very limited; practically nothing!" was the reply. "System development progressed without a hitch, and the transition was smooth." The LAN manufacturer helped make the project successful. For instance, the use of a graphic tablet at the workstation level to avoid keyboard (KB) input was suggested by the manufacturer.

According to the management of the financial institution, not only did the PC and LAN implementation eliminate the wall between the computer power and the end user but also flexibility was increased by an order of magnitude. Quite importantly, rather than make the mainframe's applications software obsolete, PCs and LAN helped extend its useful life. This made the transition much easier than it might have been. The big machine stays in place, and that is compatible with the PC and LAN concept. While the mainframe works batches and backs up the files, the user looks at a dedicated PC and communicates with other users through the LAN. All this is transparent to the user because the whole operation is automated.

The bank's total database is on the mainframe, but even if the central equipment is out of order for, say, 3 or 4 hours, the operations can go on through the PC. Total reliability is far superior to that of the mainframe alone.

Once again, let's go over the lessons which have been learned in the development and implementation of the new information systems policy. As management properly emphasized, there is no doubt that:

- The advantages presented by technology cannot be effectively exploited without user participation.
- To develop an information system for the end users, all employees must understand what the system is and also what it can do.

Once these two conditions are met, what remains is largely mechanical. The machines are available; the concepts are in evolution; and the resulting systems are simpler, easier, less costly, and more reliable than anything we had before.

Strategic Planning and Personal Computers

From an applications standpoint, it is proper to examine the developing partnership between manufacturers and users. Because of the declining cost of computer power, the information processing industry is undergoing a profound transformation. In the new directions of IS implementation, however, the interests of vendors and implementors converge rather than diverge, at least in the early stages of development.

As the case of the financial institution which we have been examining helps demonstrate, customers have begun to buy PCs in large numbers. They are attracted by the far lower cost of PCs than for other equipment and the convenience in using PCs for dedicated applications. From a vendor's viewpoint, the new markets are for:

1. Office automation
2. Personal computers
3. Software and services

Items 1 and 2 practically mean data and word processing (DP/WP) integration, and the challenge is interconnection. Whether in a financial, business, or industrial environment, workstations must communicate. They do so through LANs. As in the way the American bank in London implemented it, a LAN facility covers a limited geographical area and interconnects different types of workstations—particularly microcomputer-based devices. How wide the local area is depends substantially on LAN architecture: from 110 yards (100 meters) to nearly 6.2 miles (10 kilometers).

Personal computers, linked together through a LAN, can serve the client more effectively than any other solution provided so far. This is just as beneficial to the equipment manufacturer; we have an example of what can happen to stand-alone equipment in the story of the word processor and its shrinking market share. In the LAN and PC field, only a few years old but dynamic and fast growing, new technologies from small firms rival those from billion dollar corporations.

The features, prices, and technology of microcomputers and a LAN are distributed across a broad spectrum. Leading the trend toward a new environment are:

1. The function-packed workstation
2. The prevailing lower prices per device
3. Management's drive for productivity

Those three factors have helped the unit sales volume to explode. In line with the greater cost-effectiveness, a PC can do more than a word processor but costs only one-fourth as much. The calculator story is repeated: In the early 1970s an electronic calculator that cost $20 could do the same things as the $4000 monster of the late 1960s.

The coming changes in computers will have an even greater impact on the key industry players—greater than the switch 30 years ago from electromechanical calculators to electronic data processing. Yet only recently has it become clear that computer companies must revise their product and marketing strategies. Just to maintain their market shares, they must change radically.

If the computer, word processor, and terminal manufacturers don't meet the challenge, there are reasons to believe that the communications companies will do just that. Beginning in 1981, AT&T allocated less than 50 percent of its budget to capital investment and 28 percent to systems and stations for the end user. The latter had classically been in the 8 to 10 percent range.

It is the mainframers that have been slow moving, and this too may be changing. For many years they were lulled into complacency by the conviction that their customers were locked in by a huge investment in software that would run solely on their equipment. That is why they allowed small competitors to grow into industry giants at their expense:

- Minicomputer makers including Digital Equipment, Data General, Hewlett-Packard, and Tandem
- Word processing vendors such as Wang and Datapoint
- Personal computer outfits such as IBM (!), Apple, Tandy and many others

Micros and supermicros are attracting business users, particularly so now that a great deal of software is being developed for the first-time user and for managers.

Now that 32-bit microprocessors featuring mainframe computing power are available in tiny packages (32-bit architecture), the user can look for micromainframes to be sitting right at his or her desk in a few years. The idea of virtual memory operating systems in these small units will, in the future, become a standard because of the power of the chip and the cheapness of the memory.

What we see happening, in marketing terms, is the classical computer hardware and software business being squeezed out of existence. Users are buying prepackaged micro software that they don't have to modify. Gains in both portability and reliability have increased the feasibility of reusing software in place of re-creation and reworking. Furthermore, *fourth-generation languages not only make end user programming feasible but support impressive productivity in professional computer programming.*

While hardware technology was making great progress, software creation remained a largely manual operation. We can no longer afford to play the manual game; both cost-effectiveness and implementation timetables suffer too greatly. The rules have changed. Today software sells hardware. *The trend is toward selecting the software and then asking what kind of computer—mainframe, mini, or micro—it runs on.*

That is a long way from past practices; users customarily selected the computer first. Today more and more users look first for the software that will do the job they need done. Then they shop for the hardware they will need to make the best use of that software. At the same time, PC-to-mainframe links are becoming important. Communicating between mainframes and micros greatly expands the ways in which mainframes and PCs also are used.

A lot of processing classically done on mainframes is shuttled off to remote sites. The mainframes become big communications switches and managers of large databases. Machines of different sizes are combined in a network. Workstations provide the end user with data processing support and with graphics; the information is called up from the mainframe.

Convincing Arguments

The discussion in the preceding sections focused on the position taken by the management of a leading bank. What was the bottom line on the assistance given by workstations? How reliable was the PC solution?

Several other key questions might be asked, but those two are particularly worth asking. In answer to the first question, the bank management has stated that the intelligent workstations made it possible, for the first time, to know precisely what was done Forex operation by Forex operation through a reconcilable information flow. This statement was all the more remarkable because, as already explained, the bank had had a centralized realtime operation in place years before the PC and LAN system was implemented.

The second question followed up the first and concerned the dependability of the solution. The management answer was that the control procedures were more dependable with the PCs and LANs than with nonintelligent terminals and mainframes. So was the assurance that a deal was being carried out correctly.

Also, the second reply emphasized that how well the controls are established is a function of how well the needed controls are integrated into the banking procedures. That, in turn, depends on how well the whole organization works. For instance, in the case of geographically decentralized foreign exchange operations, it is conceivable that there is in each branch a LAN which communicates with the Forex office and general accounting at headquarters and transmits every operation. But whether this or a different solution is preferred depends on how the bank is organized and also on management preferences.

Something similar can be said of security assurance. To restrict access to the local database (at the LAN level) management can give one password to the clerical person and a different password to an officer. The latter with his password can authorize the payment. Once authorized, the payment is transmitted through the corresponding bank's LAN to the mini or mainframe the other bank is using as computing equipment. This transmission is assisted by the fact that more communications packages are available with PCs than they ever were with mainframes or minis. The choice of data communications speed-conditioned by the gateway, the modem, and the lines ranges from 300 baud to 2.4 kBPS (kilobits per second).

From a design standpoint, the flexibility of the approach is such that it has become much more feasible than in the past to develop common software. As Figure 11 shows, the basis for interbank collaboration may become much more solid than ever before. Each financial institution—A and B in this example—can have its own strategic planning, information system plan, project description, and user meetings and then use PC and LAN flexibility to integrate developments at the level of project formalization, design reviews, and results.

Another question to be asked concerns the type and nature of coming applications. Here the answer is that, now that feasibility has been demonstrated so effectively, many other departments look forward to PC and LAN implementation. The LAN-and-PC–based systems will continue to expand. Among the new areas of application are:

- Commercial effects
- Funding dealers
- Loans

All three are under development in the bank discussed in this chapter, and different areas of use have been found in other financial institutions. For instance, the Chemical Bank in New York City uses Apples as teller stations on a Cluster/One LAN with two graphic tablets per micro: one for the teller and the other for the client. This solution replaces the teller terminal, and the customer-oriented graphic tablet is used for signature verification. The latter is an application that mainframes have not been able to master in spite of much higher costs and some 16 years of realtime practice.

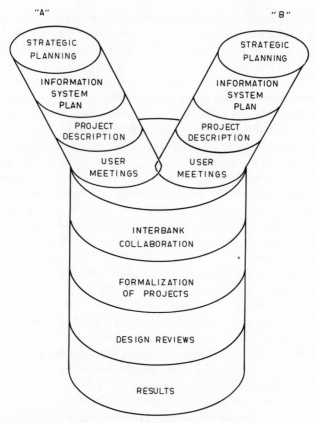

FIGURE 11. The basis for interbank collaboration may become much more solid than ever before.

Chemical and many other banks are using PCs and LANs to meet management's own decision making needs and handle electronic mail (Email) messages. "I have an Apple in my office," said the senior vice president during the London meeting. "When my people want to talk to me, they don't need to interrupt me or go through the secretary. I can talk to them through the 'messenger,' without seeing them, by looking at my message screen."

That approach also characterizes communication with headquarters. "For New York we no longer use the telex. We go through WP, the LAN/PC system," management has reported. That has become feasible because the bank integrated the LAN and PC system with:

- Interoffice mail
- Mainframe- and mini-based computer resources

In that way the system now moves into the next applications area of the treasury—the money markets—and from there into bonds and stocks (which are on PCs but not yet on the LAN) and uses a floppy disk for data transmission.

"The benefits," management reports, "are significant. It used to be that for big deposits we first made the deal and then we calculated whether we had made or lost money. Now that we have the personal computer, we get all possible results *prior* to commitment." *After all, planning, organizing and controlling is what management is all about.*

Technical Notes

Computer designations from *lap held* to *supermicro* continue to proliferate; a 1985 Radio Shack computer catalog offered pocket, portable, business, multiuser, and personal computers. There are, of course, important differences in hardware, software, size, and machine capacities, but for the nonspecialist they tend to blur. One difficulty is that development has been too rapid for language to keep pace: The first—and very crude—personal computer was being readied for market only 10 years before the Radio Shack catalog was going to press.

The term *realtime* came along with the mainframe computer; it meant immediate access to the resource. Since then it has come to be roughly synonymous with "at the same time," or "very short deadline." It might, for example, mean receiving and processing data in sufficient time to influence an activity being monitored.

CHAPTER 7

A Computer-Based Workstation

If something is not the solution, it is part of the problem.

POPULAR WISDOM

Computer-based workstations are designed for information workers. An *information worker* is anybody who generates, processes, or distributes pieces of information. All managers and also professionals, teachers, lawyers, bankers, consultants, and analysts and most of the secretaries, clerks, and salespeople fall within this definition.

The jobs that information workers do have recently been revolutionized by the new communications and computer technology, though some have preferred not to notice it. Those who refused to notice it have fallen behind in their professional standing; those who did take notice of it have moved ahead.

The history of communications started with the spoken word (roughly 40,000 B.C.) and moved ahead with the written word (3500 B.C.). About 2000 years later science awakened, made a major step forward with book printing (A.D. 1450), telecommunicated the spoken word (telephony in 1876), merged mathematics with the written word and mass-produced both of them (computers in 1946), and moved into personal computing (circa 1981).

With every new development, those left behind have been the illiterate lot. They could speak but not write, write but not read the works of others, read but not telecommunicate, telecommunicate but not compute. Then as now, the illiterate lot was destined to fade away in oblivion.

Personal computing is done at the workstation—most specifically, the intelligent, programmable workstation (WS). The physical workstation is a visual display unit containing a single-board computer dedicated to the application being executed by the user; it includes disk storage, communications devices, and other I/O media.

To many, "workstation" has a meaning strictly related to hardware. It is applied to a set of components enhanced by local computing power. That is only partially true. The *logical workstation* is the address of all input, local storage (microfiles), personal computing, and output operations. The logical and physical characteristics collectively define the functions a WS can support.

The functionality of a workstation is the sum of the functions which the WS can perform either in a stand-alone or in a networking mode. Within a communications environment, a WS can be the sender and/or receiver of messages in text, data, graphics, image, or voice form.

Goals for Workstations

In the personal computer (PC) man has created an active, intellectual partner that can be used to produce a whole new range of supports when put to work in an imaginative way. The advantages of microelectronics are low cost, high speed, low energy consumption, and high reliability, flexibility, and maintainability. The potential of this technology is now well known: labor saving, capital saving, and energy saving.

In the middle 1970s the term *executive workstation* would not have implied anything more than a desk, a calculator, and a dictating machine. But times have changed. Personal computers, spreadsheets, and packages that produce a range of aids from financial planning to color graphics have required an entirely new definition. The workstation has become much more than at-hand electronics.

Intelligent workstations are vital office elements that provide both quick access to information and the means of manipulating it. Both resources are crucial to the discharging of an executive's responsibilities. That is why the individual, intelligent workstation is a fundamental part of information systems and daily work at large. The statement is valid for all levels in an organization: executives, managers, professionals, secretaries, and clerical workers. Already some employees have more than one PC—one at work, one at home.

The PC technology has the ability to change the structure and viability of our banks, industries, offices—even farms and homes. The problem is that in many cases science and technology are moving faster than our ability to assimilate them, and that is true also of the design characteristics we would like to give to the new tools at our disposal.

The objective in WS implementation is to use microprocessor power in order to promote:

1. Human factors leading to greater productivity
2. User-friendly interfaces
3. High reliability and availability
4. Growth through design flexibility
5. Local replacement of component units—rather than massive upsets
6. Short development times
7. Easier maintenance
8. Standard and yet personalized solutions
9. Better protection of sensitive data
10. Relatively low cost per workstation
11. Ability to use many useful packages now available for microcomputers
12. Greater efficiency through the implementation of advanced technology

Organizations that use PC workstations and means of communication supported by both local area networks (LANs) and long-haul connections stay closer to the forefront of technology than do those that use minis or mainframes. Many new developments in decisions support systems, color, graphics, computer-assisted learning, input methods (such as the mouse and the graphic tablet), touch-sensitive screens, voice recognition and response, and the new database management systems (DBMS) are occurring in the PC area.

Most important of all, however, is the analytical capability that PC workstations make feasible. Executives often get where they are because of their analytical abilities, but on the job they rarely use them because they lack the right tools. That is the number 1 issue when we talk of workstations. Analytical capability is served through personal computing.

Next in importance is communications. To busy executives, who spend most of their time communicating, the advantages of online workstations should be obvious. They can avoid time-consuming telephone tag because electronic messaging allows a lot more efficient communication. Yet electronic mail is an unwise strategy unless there is a *critical mass* of online systems. Only then can there be a communications facility that executives will really want to use.

The third most important facility is databasing. A personal database, or microfile, should be at the PC level—typically hard-disk-based and eventually integrating laser disk capability in a multicommunications aggregate. Resident line disciplines should see to it that the microfile communicates with big databases by downloading and upline dumping in a way totally transparent to the user. The files in this database should be structured as messages for which the format of the now standardized North American Presentation Level Protocol Syntax (NAPLPS) is the best choice. The content of structured formats may itself be structured or unstructured. Both types can be created, corrected, and controlled through the workstation.

Figure 12 presents the logical component parts of a workstation. Depending on WS implementation, the interactive demands or the input

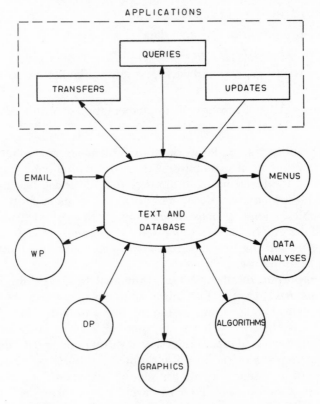

FIGURE 12. The logical component parts of a workstation.

sequences will dominate. The text and database (TDB) and the data communications facilities are an integral part of this approach.

The development of computerized analysis procedures since the middle 1960s has been largely oriented toward an increased analytic function. This has meant that access to specific capabilities and ease of use are only now becoming user concerns. Hence the emerging new technologies for input, display, and their interaction, when applied to the professional workstation, will be increasingly important.

At the output stage, the WS can be used to select and reformat information prepared by the analysis programs. It can explore the interrelations of results from several different analyses and derive the data for a succeeding analysis in an interactive mode. A distributed WS methodology for management, engineering, and other professional functions will radically change the way analytical processes are carried out. Workstations assist the workbench in breadth and completeness of function. One question that generates debate is how many applications are needed to make the executive workstation that worthwhile. Quite evidently, electronic mail is not enough. Data analysis, text manipulation, and graphics are other basic components.

As cannot be repeated too often, applications programs should be retained on hard disk and loaded over to the central memory as called for by the user. All of them should execute within a single user operating system (OS) in the workstation. The concept of concurrent operation is to have simultaneous input, storage, processing, and output. The workstation should be receiving its input and sending its output both through the end-user-oriented local peripherals and the line discipline.

General statistics regarding document handling in company communications are reflected in Figure 13. A proper implementation of WS support is to study, establish, and then exploit the company's own statistical base. Document preparation can be at two levels of complexity:

- *Basic*—a unique video approach with interactive capability; "what you see is what you get"
- More sophisticated, with the ability to work on different *windows* each composed of one or more *paving stones*

Text can be processed in a modular way by means of a *form handler* that defines on video the *format* or *content* of the module. A more generic approach is to predefine module standards able to reject nonconforming formats proposed on a distributed basis by different offices and departments.

A serious effort to enhance executive productivity will invariably involve:

1. Procedural supports for easy input and fast output
2. Algorithms for filtering the bulk of complex data
3. Reasonably fast processing capabilities
4. Local databasing features
5. Voice and graphics add-ons
6. Dependable handling of steady, lengthy working sessions
7. User-friendly capabilities

Today, multifunction workstations offer the state of the art in user-friendly technology by preserving familiar metaphors. They present themselves to users in such a way as to mimic the operations of a traditional office so that old habits are not seriously disrupted. For example, with Xerox's 8010 information system, the *metaphors* of *opening* and *closing* letters are highly recognizable in the operation of the electronic mail function. Metaphors are also preserved with respect to the generation of *charts* and *graphs*.

Let's recapitulate: Intelligent workstations offer the executive, the

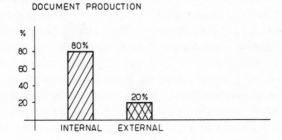

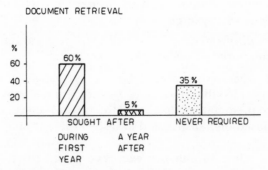

FIGURE 13. Document handling in company communications.

professional, the secretary, or the clerk desk-level computer-based supports that no other system has assured so far. The basic goals are to:

- Provide uniform input, processing, and output by enforcing standards
- Improve product and service quality
- Extend the decision-making capability
- Reduce lead time and eliminate "classical" delays
- Relieve skilled people from doing routine work
- Ease the task of maintaining and retrieving accurate documentation

Although the range of WS implementation, already wide, keeps expanding with accumulated experience, the office-type activities most influenced by workstations are graphical presentation, word processing, text composition, document research, editing and communication of messages, telecopying, and voice communications.

Higher-Level Software

The design of workstations implies an integration of computers and communications software and hardware (SW/HW) engineering with language support and the appropriate methodology. As outlined in the preceding section, the goal should be that of providing efficient support to the workplace whether for decision making or clerical purposes.

A professional workstation can be used both to improve the efficiency by which data is collected and to assist the user in the preparation of data for a formal presentation or report. Performance can be improved through the development of user-adapted *macroprocedures* and workstation assistance in the training of both new and existing users.

In the old online concept, in which nonintelligent terminals were provided to the user, both the functions relative to the management of the terminals and the manipulation of data were handled by the central computer. Moving those functions to the terminal itself, the intelligent workstation, has led to:

- Significant increase in the quality of service
- Reduction of response time
- Improvement of system reliability

In most applications, PC workstations provide a form of computing superior to that of timesharing. The requirements of the intelligent WS, however, go well beyond the facilities provided by a local computer. They must include:

- Advantages equivalent to those of timesharing such as user-to-user communications
- The ability to share programs and databases
- The ingenuity of making WS usage a matter-of-course operation

The preferred way to implement computer-based functions is to interconnect all workstations by means of a high-speed local area network. The LAN is controlled by a distributed operating system which provides transparent access to all network resources. A network-wide virtual memory system is a good answer.

Additional WS facilities such as large virtual address space and a concurrent multiple-window display system significantly increase user productivity. A high-resolution display system with SW/HW support is an essential component. That is also true of higher-level software to better implement the man-information interface.

Higher-level software leads us to the concept of the *logical WS*, including expected input/output (I/O) control of logical operations. How they will be mapped into the physical world is an issue to be addressed by software.

Meshing necessary applications with available physical devices is only part of the challenge; another part consists of the new tasks necessary for effective implementation. As Table 11 demonstrates, they should center on:

- Specification
- Primary input
- Input control
- Data analysis
- Data synthesis
- Presentation of results

Each task imposes different demands on *information exchange, interaction rate,* and *internal processing*—the three key variables of interest at the professional workstation. It will not be an easy job to rid ourselves of the bad practices of 30 years. Yet we must now learn *to program the devices not on the basis of their functions, but on the basis of the functions of the applications we expect from them.*

This closely resembles a fundamental modern management principle that we should not base plans for the future on the resources we currently have. Instead, we should expand or contract our resources in accordance

TABLE 11   *Tasks and key variables of interest at the professional workstation*

Phase	Information exchange	Interaction rate	Internal processing
Task specification	Low	Low	Low
Primary input	High	Low	Low
Input control	Low	High	Medium
Data analysis	Low	Low	High
Data synthesis	High	High	Low
Presentation of results	Medium	Medium	Low

with the goals we wish to reach. Quite similarly, we must change our approach to storage manipulation. *We should give ourselves plenty of storage space in which we can write and effectively handle text, data, and pictures, depending on projected usage.*

Analytical computation, memory capability, and the methodology for their effective usage are the pillars on which the expert systems (E systems) effort rests. An important question is this: How much knowledge is needed for acceptable performance? Mnemonic aids can relate new data to a large existing store, and practical limits rest on voluntary search size and associated housekeeping complexity. Computation is no constraint when currently available microprocessors support nearly one million instructions per second (MIPS) at the dedicated WS level.

The development of the proper methodology does present challenges, and that is where higher-order software enters the picture. Learning must now be looked on as the accumulation of knowledge versus adjustment of parameters. *Expert problem solving is made feasible by the use of substantial knowledge.* The new tools and outlook create another avenue: executable functional specifications. These contribute to an incremental development system beyond the usual programming cycle.

A typical simple procedure may be to detect an error, stop execution, explore the machine state, fix the error by editing one or more source files, recompile, link and load, execute, and study output. Alternatively, the machine may decide to *undo* undesired actions.

A sensor system is another example of higher-order software; one application is collision warning for boats and ships. A dumb system may use Fourier transforms, different filters, correlation systems, and so on. An expert system would use knowledge about sound sources and the relationship between behavior of sources and the resulting signals.

In an expert collision avoidance system, a simple sound threshold device could give proximity warning while signal processing algorithms yielded such information as harmonic structure, direction, signal characteristics, and signal association. Humans use such information for signal analysis, the formation of an opinion, and subsequent situation estimates. Expert systems are trainable in a few months in such human functions.

While these may not be immediate goals for expert system implementation, their projected implementation by the end of the decade demands that currently designed systems be open-ended and that the study of WSs takes them into account as future modules. Prior to 1990, we can expect to have at our disposal a machine that can read and understand a whole library—and let's not forget that research is currently in progress on self-reproducing systems.

Computer-based expert systems are capable of oil exploration, fault diagnosis, algebraic programming, function scheduling and other machine configuration, and diagnosis. The latter class of applications has so far included automotive systems, electronics, and medicine.

Higher-order software needs an overstructure, a main structure, and an understructure as shown in Figure 14. These three layers will be served both by software and by hardware. Provided we have clear ideas about what we wish to achieve, supporting these structures poses no problems, because very large scale integration (VLSI) promises up to 500,000 components for a few dollars. However, let's note that the basic building blocks will no longer be gates, or multipliers, but units capable of speech synthesis, probabilistic reasoning, and so on. With time and experience:

- Off-the-shelf knowledge banks with thousands of rules will appear.
- Current applications will use only a few hundred rules easily stored on a single chip.

Chip vendors are now working to develop these larger building blocks in expert systems. Such systems will become as transportable and marketable as books and software. They will:

1. Present knowledge in an organized but adaptable manner
2. Support knowledge in terms familiar to end users
3. Employ user-friendly interface functions
4. Exploit the kinds of reasoning which are available

The functional capabilities of knowledge-based systems will include an *external view* for consultation and the creation of knowledge banks and an *internal view* enabling the use of knowledge, inference, and the following of rules. Analysis in such systems will be based on thorough

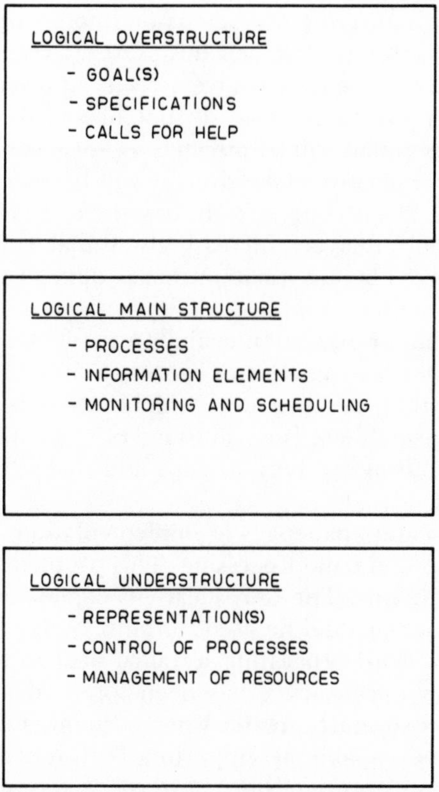

```
┌─────────────────────────────────────────┐
│  LOGICAL OVERSTRUCTURE                   │
│                                          │
│      - GOAL(S)                           │
│      - SPECIFICATIONS                     │
│      - CALLS FOR HELP                     │
│                                          │
│                                          │
│                                          │
└─────────────────────────────────────────┘

┌─────────────────────────────────────────┐
│  LOGICAL MAIN STRUCTURE                  │
│                                          │
│      - PROCESSES                         │
│      - INFORMATION ELEMENTS              │
│      - MONITORING AND SCHEDULING         │
│                                          │
│                                          │
│                                          │
└─────────────────────────────────────────┘

┌─────────────────────────────────────────┐
│  LOGICAL UNDERSTRUCTURE                  │
│                                          │
│      - REPRESENTATION(S)                 │
│      - CONTROL OF PROCESSES              │
│      - MANAGEMENT OF RESOURCES           │
│                                          │
│                                          │
│                                          │
└─────────────────────────────────────────┘
```

FIGURE 14. The need for an overstructure, a main structure, and an understructure for higher-order software.

understanding of the problem domain. In principle, there is no general intelligence process. Without a knowledge bank, no algorithm will suffice.

There are, however, some areas in which it is not advisable to apply expert systems. They typically include functions that are currently performed adequately, are predictably cost-effective, and are troublefree. We will see specific examples in the following section.

Looking at Implementation Requirements

Although the discussion of higher-order software is intended for orientation, it is nonetheless true that there are at present many SW/HW tools that were not available only a few years ago. Given adequate training, such tools can be put to use immediately.

113

Managers are discovering how hands-on interaction with computers gives them special insights into their businesses. Executive workstations equipped with mice or touch-sensitive screens to insert commands are making it easy for executives who do not like to use a keyboard. In time, intelligent terminals will be directed by voice commands. Furthermore, as younger executives take over, it will become common to see them working on PCs. Some already use them to take advantage of their power as tools that are increasingly available at very low cost. Others use their WSs for information that is difficult to retrieve otherwise.

Hence, to dismiss workstation evolution as idle fancy is about equal to the foresight of a late nineteenth century editorialist for the *London Times* who wrote that the then new telephones would not come into common use because "there is no shortage of messengers in England." Intelligent workstations are here to stay, and that's the way they have to be approached.

One of the greater challenges in implementation is the integration of word processing and data processing. This problem is still wide open to imaginative solutions. The only clear-cut commandment is that the same physical devices should be used for both kinds of jobs. It is highly wasteful to have a word processing terminal next to a data processing terminal, although that practice has been followed in some quarters. The waste appears so much greater when account is taken of the great number of products capable of supporting both functions.

Integration has its prerequisites, however. A serious study must first focus on the need to identify the time absorbed during the working day by the activities relevant to the workpost to be automated. This study must be both qualitative and quantitative.

For instance, the study for a secretarial level job will be concerned with typing, correspondence handling, answering the telephone, archiving, photocopying, and so on. Having established the main activities, it is important to quantify (in percent) how much each of them is dedicated to preparatory and elaboration tasks that can be handled locally and which of them involve exchange of information with other offices.

Records have a modular structure in a word processing system. Paragraphs and even figures must be related, sequenced, and updated through the database facility. Keyword indexes in document retrieval need updating. The ability to merge graphics information with records can facilitate many applications. The merging of text and data helps both in producing reports and in forming letters.

A finer study will permit subdivision of the time attributed to a certain task, such as typing, into subclasses: memos, creative correspondence, standard letters, studies and reports of many pages, offers and contracts, forms and tables. The subdivision should always reflect the necessity to consult an archive. Part and parcel of the finer study is the management of paper archives present in the office, with attention to the type and volume of the archive itself and the frequency of consultation.

Word processing and graphics production applicable to both management and clerical users is expected to show significant growth. Comparison of usage current in the middle 1980s with that expected within the following few years did not suggest major shifts in applications. As already stated:

- The current job needs to be both qualified and quantified.
- The new applications perspectives must be thoroughly studied.
- The door must be left open for the incorporation of impressive developments like those identified with expert systems.

A similar type of grid analysis is clearly possible for executive functions which are more specific to the job. For instance, in a banking environment, executive function may focus on general accounting and analytic accounting, liquidity analysis, profit and loss evaluation, risk evaluation procedures, current and actual comparison for budgetary control, and simulation planning.

An example can help explain the level to which a study concerning a given application must be carried. The current and actual comparison for budgetary control will typically include evaluation of current expenditures, evaluation of current intake and employment of funds, change analysis considering, say 2 years of exercise, comparison with other organizations over the current time period, and simulation planning for the next four periods, whether months or years.

Experimentation can be carried out nicely at the WS level, and simulation is the most important tool. It offers the executive context, direction, and alarm signals. In every case, an able answer to the established requirements must use the best that current technology can offer. It should embody two viewpoints (Figure 15):

1. Demands posed by management
2. Basic considerations at the user end

Management demands include continuity, reliability, comprehensive approaches, cost, and system performance. They also pose a user system performance requirement detailed as response time, ease of use, interactive tutorials, and help, prompts, and forgiveness for faults in manipulation.

Workstations call not only for an ingenious, properly documented

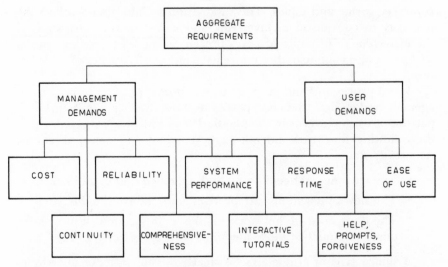

FIGURE 15. An able answer to the established requirements must embody two viewpoints: demands posed by management and basic considerations at the user end.

design but also for babysitting provisions. Installations initially experience higher than expected WS failure rates if no hand-holding provisions are made. And although hand-holding usually concerns the applications aspect(s), other failures may be caused by a combination of power line surges, mechanical shock, and static electricity.

With proper planning the logical and physical problems can easily be solved at the source. Failure to think ahead can cause delays, friction, failures, and higher costs. But although both the physical and the logical components of a workstation network must be attacked at an early date, the latter of the two will pose by far the greater challenges.

From that comes the interest in thorough research prior to WS implementation. In the research, careful account should be taken of the fact that most of the information elements necessary in an organization are particularly valuable in one location. An estimated 75 to 90 percent of the data used in a local environment is generated within that environment. Quite similarly, some 75 to 90 percent of the information produced within a local environment is typically used within that environment. That is, the majority of communications are local:

- The largest proportion of information used within a department has limited value outside that department.
- Most information exchange takes place within a relatively limited organizational area.

A substantial part of local processing is interactive in nature and bursty. A similar statement can be made about *file transfers* from one database to another. Whether transmitting text and data files or high-resolution graphics, the system requires lots of channel capacity approximating the speed of a computer input/output (I/O) bus. In handling high-volume traffic, message routing and network control should introduce as little delay as possible and so provide speedy access to the database for all nodes and users.

Furthermore, in implementing office automation and decision support systems, we must start from the areas carrying the greater weight: An estimated 75 percent of office costs is attributable to the managerial and professional personnel and only 12 percent to secretarial assistance. Emphasis should therefore be placed on mental (managerial) productivity.

Problems with Office Automation

Distributed workstations that provide personal computing, supporting microfiles, and communications capabilities can bring to all organizations that care to use them abundant and low-cost intellectual power. Yet it is just as true that, wherever we turn, the potential of the computer age has not been realized. We are still scratching the surface.

That makes planning more difficult. Most companies can understand that both their daily operations and their future depend on collecting and interpreting data, transmitting the data to computers, analyzing, and reaching conclusions. But they fail to see what comes next, and therefore they are ill-prepared for the future.

The first and most serious problem with office automation, intelligent workstations, and communicating databases is that *concepts and strategy are often missing.*

- Not all companies have a clear concept of their goals in terms of advanced technology.
- Therefore, they cannot formulate a *competitive* strategy.
- This handicaps them in setting objectives and making budgetary evaluations.

The second major problem is the *lack of the needed knowhow* to undertake the studies necessary for successful implementation. Specialists with skills in advanced technology are in very short supply. Furthermore, a consistent effort must be made to convert to the new distributed computer-based capabilities not only the specialists but also the users.

That is particularly important when we talk of managerial productivity. Office automation at large and, most specifically, intelligent workstations are going nowhere unless most senior executives and middle managers use workstations as everyday tools. Only when most executives, middle managers, and professionals start using the microprocessor-based workstations of the automated office will the subjects of which we are talking come alive. Workstations are no longer expensive, but training a vast group of diversified individuals is a complex, complicated task.

Of all three difficulties, training is the biggest. Training concerns people. Only training and use can make evident the fact that the executive level workstation allows the senior manager:

- To access instantaneously the information processed by subordinates
- To communicate with subordinates and with peers

And if the senior executive needs more assistance, he or she can get it from the terminal itself.

Training seminars, though a necessity in an age of rapid change, have not yet been planned as they should be. The need is not filtering down the organization fast enough—even with allowance for the dramatic requirements. It is estimated that an engineer's knowledge becomes obsolete every 5 years. Within the same time frame the banker loses 50 percent of his professionality.

By 1990 the average adult professional will need some type of steady retraining. In the Bell System, the solution goes by the name of Teletraining. This is a way to deliver course work from a central, instructor-controlled location to one or more remote sites by means of audio services, graphic equipment, and telephone lines. Unlike broadcasting, Teletraining is interactive at all times. Participants in all the connected locations can speak to or hear one another simultaneously. Teletraining can be effectively combined with laser disk implementation. PC functionality, with hard disk and laser disk support plus data communications protocols, can form an *interactive videodisk* which has a great many profitable implementations—training being one of them.

Such interactive video information systems integrate commercial videodisk technology with computers. They demonstrate document-handling capabilities; for they are capable of packaging 500 Mbytes on one videodisk. That is the equivalent of about 400,000 pages of text and data at a cost of $17 per laser disk and less than $1000 per laser read-only unit.

A third key problem is *divided procurement.* In most organizations, procurement responsibility is split among management information systems and data processing (MIS/DP), office equipment (typewriters, copiers), and telephone services. No clear-cut lines exist, nor does the needed coordination. Yet a valid division is straightforward. It will give MIS/DP the responsibility for any equipment which has a microprocessor, random-access memory (RAM), disk storage, and data communications capabilities and is programmable.

Way down the list comes a fourth problem: *handling aging applications.* * In principle, there are three ways to treat them:

1. One is to rewrite them on microcomputers by using professional services.

In a significant number of DP applications, much of the activity is personal or local and can best be executed at the workplace. But rewriting should not be done blindly. The application must first be revamped and redimensioned and then programmed in a fourth-generation language (4GL)—preferably a database-oriented system.

2. The second approach is to let the end user take care of the problem on his WS.

The WS will typically be a PC with spreadsheet or integrated software. Many DP applications running on mainframes can be handled interactively through spreadsheets, and such a solution will help improve productivity, reduce mainframe workload, and provide faster access to text and data.

User programming through a 4GL is even more welcome because PC installations are expected to grow in all dimensions and the most dramatic growth is related to the substitution of PC power for the mainframe. Offloading small programs and related data from the main computer should be promoted.

3. A new generation of PCs now being brought to the market begins to approach mainframe program portability.

A good example is IBM's PC 370. It is well, however, to remember that aging 370 mainframe applications must be of a size that can fit on a microcomputer. New programs also will be needed. If this prediction is correlated with the fact that the majority of PC users are expected to be management personnel, we can expect an increase in the demand for management decision support applications.

---

* Aging computer applications have outlived their useful life cycles and/or they feature inordinate software maintenance costs.

The fact that so much is expected of PCs in the area of replacing programs currently run on mainframes may explain the willingness of DP managers to move along with the personal workstation revolution. That is true despite the misperception that the PC erodes the MIS/DP manager's power base. In the end, distributed intelligence through interactive workstations and expert system implementation will necessitate a new order of organization, whether MIS/DP management likes it or not. It will oblige us to design new tools, change the capabilities of our services, and multiply the effectiveness of our personnel. It will have great impact on every business.

Technical Notes

Expert systems, like more rudimentary computer programs, are a means of solving problems with computer software and hardware. What has changed is the nature of the problems we want solved. The early computer was a procedural device, which means that the path it had to follow to solve a problem, say, a computation, had to be explained to it algorithmically, step by step. This was done by means of a programming language. Originally, the *programming language* was very nearly the machine code. Then symbolic programming was developed by means of assemblers, a means of specifying both operations and groups of locations by using symbols. The third generation of programming languages (1957–1958) were Cobol, Fortran, PL/1, and the like, which enabled the user to program the machine with instructions in something like normal speech.

The fourth generation (4GL) comprises nonprocedural languages: from spreadsheets and integrated software to precompilers, shells of system commands, and so on. The 4GL implies the use of where-from and how-to rules rather than detailed steps. Typically the machine is programmed by form and examples—what the user sees is what he gets.

The next, fifth generation of programming languages will be based on expert systems. This will be the first practical application of artificial intelligence. We have to apply more expertise to solve problems intelligently; and from an end user's viewpoint, it is much easier to interact and converse with an intelligent system, one that "thinks" in something of the way we do.

In our higher intellectual processes we work with facts, relations between those facts, and methods for using the relations to solve problems. So do expert systems. They can be inductive; they can develop their own rules and methods as they need them. Alternatively, they may be deductive. The rules are assigned in advance by the developer and kept dynamic by the system.

The *knowledge bank* is not a database in the data processing sense of the word; it is a knowledge base including the expert system's rules and methodology. These create an inference engine which possesses significant expertise and intelligence in a well-defined (hence limited) domain of knowledge. The expert system depends on its knowledge bank for giving advice and, most important, for documenting the advice.

CHAPTER 8

The Managerial Viewpoint

Three may keep a secret, if two of them are dead.

POOR RICHARD'S ALMANAC

The fact that personal computer (PC) solutions are available to people with problems at their workplaces advances in a number of ways the effort to implement data and word processing (DP/WP) integration. The new system should comprise a series of components for creating, editing, filing, and retrieving documents. It should support computing, include a broad line of graphics equipment, and provide text and data sending via telephone lines.

Most important, an integrated DP/WP system should address total office productivity by allowing managers and professionals to store, share, and access the information upon which their executive tasks depend. This will be the essence of system design in the coming years, and because of it the sales growth of various generations of word processing products may be affected significantly. Applications will define the growth of demand, which at the time of writing had put the market in the midst of an evolutionary change away from a preponderance of hardcopy stand-alones toward display-based network systems.

Users will increasingly add telecommunications, utility programs, and other features to their word processors to save time and effort. This variety of uses will tend to blur the distinction between:

- Word processors with data processing capability
- Microcomputers that perform data handling and text editing

Statistics established through fundamental studies tend to accelerate the DP/WP merger trend. A Booz, Allen, Hamilton study, for instance, found that 90 percent of all information created in a department never goes beyond 1 kilometer (0.62 mile) from that department for storage or use. If the BAH study is worthy of credence, the next crucial step is to interconnect stand-alone workstations (WSs) within the 1-kilometer radius and create a distributed intelligence capability. That makes it possible to start with a basic system that grows by the attachment of more devices. The local area network (LAN) architecture should guarantee that performance will not be degraded by the addition of more WSs.

Critical Factors for a Managerial Workstation

The new text and data orientation will involve color and graphics, interactive approaches, common access to shared resources, a spelling dictionary, calendar services, calculator functions, filing and retrieval capability, and word and records processing. Workstations will be designed around the concept of page display and be able to handle archives. Voice facilities will address voice mail and also speech recognition, input, and synthesis—all with the major goal of increasing managerial productivity.

To judge by developments, it is important to evaluate the critical factors. Not only are DP and WP vital now, they will keep on being so well into the 1990s and will involve:

1. Personal computers
2. Distributed data processing
3. Small business systems
4. Text-handling facilities
5. Data entry methods

The mode of data entry, by 1990, will depend on voice facilities. Probably there will be no keying in. Prior to that time, an explosive increase can be expected in the number of users of computer-based teletex systems. In 1980, in the United States, an estimated 160,000 people made use of electronic mail (Email); by 1985 the number of users was expected to exceed one million; and by 1991 almost half of all white-collar workers (or 21 million) may be using Email. By then, the Email systems will have been integrated with store-and-forward voice message services and will be hooked into optical disk databases.

Until such complete systems come into existence, Email within an organization can result in savings largely because of the reduction in executive time and telephone expense involved in telephone tag. Some statistics that reflect current practices are given in Table 12.

In a recent American study of the coming merger of data, text, and voice it was found that 88 percent of users consider the DP/WP integration to be a fundamental need. The concept is to allow both voice and data operation over conventional telephone facilities; coaxial cable local networks, radio links, and so on.

To get effective support of mental productivity, system design must be steered away from past trends. The "microcomputer at every desk" should be seen in that light. Up to the early 1980s, office equipment was primarily oriented to clerks and secretaries. As such, it was basically WP and mostly batch in type. New products go well beyond that; they become the pivot of a change which is in the offing: from word processing to information retrieval.

Efficient, user-friendly, and instantaneous retrieval capabilities are a fundamental issue for people concerned with quality of information and design support. The basic services to be provided include:

1. Calendar management
2. Meetings scheduler
3. Reminder of things to do
4. Document management
5. Visual memory and fast, easy retrieval
6. Electronic messaging

TABLE 12 *Telephone tag estimates*

Outcome	Calls, %	Length, minutes
No answer or answer machine	5	1.5
Out of office	20	2.0
Out to lunch	15	1.5
In a meeting	25	1.0
On the phone	15	1.5
Not available	6	2.0
Please hold to reach party	4	12.5
Directly reaching party	10	10.0

All this is equivalent to electronic in- and out-baskets. The range of applications calls for an audio workstation with digitized information, but it also allows the user to receive "voicegrams." With such facilities, the user can dictate a message and the system will compress it and, when asked, play it back.

Significantly, the applications environment in the London bank which we considered in a preceding chapter supports the impressive range of facilities of which we are talking now. The Forex operator has voice, data, and text facilities all in an integrated unit, and teletex facilities also are present. They are supported through the "messenger service."

The executive's workstation—and in the current implementation there are sixty-five of them—incorporates three video units: a scratchpad, a reporter, and a messenger. Through the graphic tablet, the executive writes on the scratchpad, and this is revocable till the cursor is put on the "deal" command. The executive selects the needed reports and views them through the second video. And messages—whether internal or external—are received through the third unit.

It is quite evident that an understructure must be developed on both the technical and the managerial sides. The latter should include control procedures adapted to respond in an effective manner to the new environment.

Control Procedures to Please the Auditors

Although the technology of a system may be wonderful, the rules of a financial institution see to it that management tends to withhold full support until the controllers are convinced that the new system can operate without flaws. It is, therefore, proper to take a look at the controllers' reaction prior to elaborating in greater detail on the way the system works.

Again with reference to the American bank in London, the senior vice president has said that, for control purposes, the solution to be adopted was discussed with the controllers when the PC and LAN system was still in the design stages. It was agreed that control was to be postmortem. A system of checks and balances was therefore instituted to see to it that the error probability was reduced well below the level reached with mainframes or even minis. The reason is simple: Fewer people are involved in the steps subsequent to a deal's confirmation, and so the possibility of error is lessened.

Data entry, verification, database update, and data communications enter this equation. The local area network plays a key role. An end user who has just a stand-alone PC must access the mainframe for data. But if the application involves a LAN, the need for data, text, and image is met locally.

In a systems project based on PCs, and LAN the whole range of security must be considered: the eventuality of an improper use of facilities, disclosure or modification of information, loss of resources, and so on. The design should provide for requirements and constraints, policy issues, implementation, basic considerations of entry to certain areas such as the database and journal, access routes, records, and logs.

In an implementation in which I was involved, the identification of system components received proper attention: machine-sensible identification, defining and identifying users and WSs, and defining and identifying all system components: software, hardware, data files, printers, and documentation. Evaluation included the ways and means to be used for monitoring, recognition of violations, utility of trend analysis, systems reliability, user accessibility to system information, possible vulnerability of database, integrity constraints, audit tools, and audit trails. Vulnerability was evaluated by the controller's department.

An example of a procedure established jointly by foreign operators and controllers is the limit put on the deals a Forex operator can make. This has been elaborated for better control. Another example is the electronic signature through putting the cursor on "deal," together with unique identification of the individual station. Still another is the post-mortem ticket printed on the LAN's online facility and countersigned. Spot and forward, Eurocurrencies, deposits, and deadlines—all are handled in a secure manner, and mistakes are immediately identified. The advantage of a LAN is that one does not have to wait for the long mainframe reaction.

This question was posed during a working meeting: "When you advance a loan to a client for foreign exchange, what sort of mismatch do you get?" The executive who asked the question added that only after a year of pressure did he get the listing he needed to check for possible discrepancies.

"I had the same problem," answered a senior vice president. "But no more. Now with the computer I have it myself." It was further said that among the advantages of the immediate response was the squaring out of accounts.

The coinvolvement of the controllership is, parenthetically, one of the pillars on which the new developments in electronic banking rest. And since electronic banking is the way of the future, the better we do our homework, the more solid the system will be. "We stress electronic banking because we are convinced that only those banks which go ahead can survive," said the senior vice president. "The advantages over those who stay behind are many."

For a financial institution, as for any other firm, the business opportunity has to be properly evaluated. That requires good answers to key questions: What's the strategy? The products we offer to the market? The drive of the markets themselves? The applications sectors? The hidden costs? The risks? The opportunities? The profitability?

Today banks spend a lot of money on communications pathways, computer-based databases, and office automation in general because that's their competitive edge. So much the better when the work is done the right way and it improves service, enhances controllability, and reduces costs.

The Change in Approach by DP Management

Although most banks and industrial companies have not yet established a policy on PCs, the situation is that DP management must now change its attitude. "Change its attitude" means "think small," use technology the wise way, and get involved with PCs and LANs before everybody in the organization starts using PCs independently. As the case we have considered clearly demonstrates, an ingenious PC and LAN implementation can make DP a focal point for the new technology. At the same time, it can provide a real service to the users.

There are functional reasons for the push in the PC and LAN direction, the substitution of hardcopy being just an example. As Table 13 suggests, in the absence of online softcopy implementation, the projected paper jungle will be impossible to manage in a few years. What better

TABLE 13 Projected paper jungle without online softcopy implementation

Subject	U.S. market, $ billion		Possible annual growth, %
	1980	1985	
Multicopy			
Continuous modules	2.63	19.00	14.1
Free-standing modules	1.29	5.83	10.6
Single-copy modules	0.51	0.71	2.2
Checks	0.60	2.00	8.3
Other banking forms	0.35	0.43	1.5
Envelopes	1.38	3.68	6.8

example of PC and LAN wisdom can there be than a sharp improvement in that direction?

There are, of course, a goodly number of prerequisites to be observed. A basic one is systems analysis, and we will return to it. Equally important are the design studies. Whether in the office or in the factory, the PC and LAN approach requires that:

1. The system be *object-based*
2. The *nodes* with memory and processing power be well defined
3. The *protocols* exist for tasks running on one node to access the other
4. The *programs* be systemwide, rather than for a specific machine

Above all, there must be a *strategy*: Where do we wish to go? What is it that we want to reach? At what cost? Within which timetable?

Having found good answers to those questions, we must look at the mechanics: How can we simulate the complete system which we project? What's the experiment to be used at each WS? How much memory shall we put at each node? Many answers are possible in each situation, but basic definitions are enough to serve as guidelines:

- With the *PC and LAN*, the main consideration is *not* the central processing unit (CPU) cycles but access to disk.
- Thus it may be advantageous that the *database* is distributed to a *number of nodes* which can store it.
- Such nodes can be like workstations or dedicated rear-end machines. What is important to the user is that there is *one logical source* of data.

From a single logical source of data arises the need for pointers to particular information elements and associated routing information. Design, development, and implementation must be such that the LAN architecture is flexible and easy to implement and maintain, the chosen protocols provide reasonable assurance of error correction and a guaranteed message delivery, and the supported *band* is wide enough to cover the projected application(s). It is equally important that the featured services meet the applications requirements cost-effectively.

The strategy should be to develop a LAN architecture which can promote lots of parallelism—and be open to future developments. The design must assure that the system we build is flexible and expandable. It is almost certain that, as applications experience accumulates, we will need to increase the number of nodes, accommodate types such as storage nodes and workstations, blur the distinction between one processor and another, and pay particular attention to end use considerations.

The WS is the real man-information interface, and therefore it is the point of our major concern. Regarding the operation of a distributed database, IBM says that 80 percent of our processing is done against 20 percent of our database. When we have properly identified the 20 percent, we can look at how to distribute it:

- Personal
- Local
- Text and data warehouse

And it is good to remember that, with LAN and long-haul networks (LHN), every distributed database (DDB) can be accessed by every WS in the system.

I have stressed these issues prior to talking of system analysis because office automation studies must be carried out from the right perspective. That being so, twelve steps are taken to find the procedural solution to be followed:

1. Identify the problem.
2. Plan the activities.
3. Establish the criteria (success/failure, cost/benefit).
4. Select a pilot group.
5. Try to understand the organization you are selecting (early/late adapters).
6. Comprehend the technology you use.
7. Involve the users in the process.
8. Replan; reevaluate; set milestones.
9. Describe the milestones to the user: results, documentation, implementors, management.
10. Implement the system and use the acquired experience in other applications that train the user properly.
11. Make the knowhow thus gained operational on a larger scale; then post-audit.
12. Babysit, maintain, and update.

Since we aim to provide a solution at the workplace, we must assure that the solution is efficient, acceptable, and advisable. Table 14 lists, by percent, customer wishes in DP/DC gear identified in a recent study. The factors judged were product quality, maintenance, sales contact, ready software, and price. (Some respondents gave more than one answer, so there is no point in adding up the columns.) Other features

TABLE 14 *Customer wishes in DP/DC gear*

	Comm. products	Data terminating equipment		Personal computers	Data entry	Graphics	Printers	Magn. periph.
		Intel.	Nonintel.					
Product quality	57*	39*	44*	48	38*	53*	42*	39*
Maintenance	48	38	30	34	23	10	34	33
Sales contact	30	12	18	13	16	10	10	14
Ready software	9	28	4	56*	14	10	3	8
Price	35	20	32	35	21	19	20	18

* Highest percent

Note: Because some respondents gave more than one answer, the columns do not add to 100%.

131

also deserve attention. If the design is specific to the manager, then the offering must:

- Have cordless equipment
- Be able to integrate communications
- Have smaller, but polyvalent, units
- Be capable of creating the message in an easy way
- Offer alternative transmission capabilities
- Be fully security-protected

Security protection means sign-on: The recipient, before reading the transferred messages, must sign on to acknowledge system access. And since the manager will be dealing with different equipment, there is also a need for a way to address all of the available communications capabilities as part of a package.

Like any new system or procedure, myriaprocessors cannot be installed overnight throughout the organization. The best advice is to contemplate group-level implementation within a 3- to 5-year time frame. The immediate objective should be to create a situation in which product use gets polished and user comfort becomes assured.

Salient Issues for Management Attention

Having discussed the new managerial workstation from the system viewpoint, we can now direct our attention to the salient problems from a decision-making point of view. What are the *three top problems* on which management must focus its attention?

Since applications programming (AP) is the interface between the computer equipment and the user, the first task prior to beginning work on a project is to answer this question: "What problem do I need to solve?" The answer must be:

- Given in a factual and documented way
- Presented in a clear written form
- Signed by the user as evidence of approval

This is the first rule of a solid software development procedure.

The second rule is to have a fundamentally correct working model for AP development. It will save much design time and even more discussion and argument. It will also improve results. At the time of writing, the Japanese were working on such a model, but the models available in Europe and in America left much to be desired in respect to both tools and methodology. The greatest failure was in formatting and formalizing the user-analyst interaction. And the remark about weak links is all the more applicable to detailed system analysis and test procedures.

Taking one step at a time, our priority is to solve problems associated with the first critical node—the interface between user and analyst. Microcomputers with graphic tablets can be instrumental in the solution if they are *dedicated* to this task. Because the device is dedicated to one single job with the goal of doing it capably, tool and methodology merge into one entity. But a caution is in order: The work must be done in an imaginative way with the result leading to an interactive application.

The third rule is to institute planning procedures. Lack of planning leads to lack of accomplishment, and then to anxiety and fear of failure. Anxiety breeds reluctance to risk making decisions which might later turn out to have been wrong. Fear of failure results in reluctance to set goals and to communicate openly about the business to be done. This creates a vicious cycle which in turn destabilizes goal setting and planning.

Again, the very first requirement is to answer the question: "What problem do I need to solve?" In technical terms, this leads to defining the information system's purposes. What we are setting out to do is not to install modems or computers. Installing equipment is the easier part of the solution, way down the line of priorities. The system's purpose comes first.

Goals should be defined and constantly kept in mind. The first has to do with the reason for the network being built. What are the major objectives? They must be defined, studied, analyzed, and reached.

Although the major objectives should be given priority in implementing a computer and communications network, it is feasible to furnish other services as well. Thus minor goals also should be set to define the gains the system can make, while serving the major purposes, at little or no extra expense.

Still another requirement is in order. A system established today to meet concrete requirements must be capable of evolution. Future new goals can be major or minor; they comprise services that a network can render the organization but for which it is not yet ready. It is important to be aware of these future possibilities, even if we are not yet ready to write either a formal analysis or an implementation timetable. Without the awareness, the computer and communications system constructed would effectively lock out future options.

Personal computers are being implemented to exchange data and programs with other PCs, minis, and mainframes. They allow the user to prepare material offline and thereby reduce communications costs and free phone lines for other uses. If a workstation is connected to a timesharing service, the use of the PC will help reduce connect-time charges and eliminate storage charges by taking advantage of the machine's own mass storage facilities. This makes the desktop PC (or rather desk-drawer PC if it is integrated into the office furniture) two machines in one.

The equipment can do double duty, unlike some of the most intelligent terminals. Online, it's a terminal; offline, it's a computer. All the user needs to convert a micro to an intelligent terminal is:

- An interface card (standard with many desk-tops)
- A telephone modem
- A smart terminal package

Most smart terminal packages offer a variety of benefits. For instance, Visiterm (from Visicorp) transmits account number and password with a single keystroke, sets the baud rate, formats the output for easy reading, and dials the number on the user's behalf. A 256-character buffer prevents the loss of characters during delays in transmission.

Yet, as already emphasized in another connection, micros have been an example of the computer professionals' backwardness. In the early 1960s, data processing (DP) professionals were agents of change, but since then they have tended to be agents of reaction and conservatism. Users have become the true computing pioneers. There are numerous examples. In the late 1960s users put on pressure for timesharing, despite DP professional skepticism. Then in the early 1970s users pioneered the mini applications. Later, when word processing arrived, many people in DP said the technology was just a jump up from electronic typewriters. And when micros appeared, the DP people said they were toys.

But just as DP professionals resisted timesharing, minis, and office automation and then became converted enthusiasts, so DP is beginning to realize the importance and user attractiveness of micros: Personal computers today mean one man–one computer, and this has a tremendously important effect on the user environment.

At the same time, as we will see in the appropriate chapters, the microcomputer cost is a critical factor to watch. The market is extremely price-sensitive. Each time a less expensive product appears:

1. It steals the show, unless the current product is firmly established in applications software.
2. The market expands; the number of microcomputer owners increases dramatically; but users want applications software support.
3. The volume of worthwhile applications balloons, and in doing so it accelerates product evolution.

Just because of this rapid development, manufacturers and vendors would be well advised to examine the markets left behind by a popular new trend, particularly the owners of older, less popular computers. This group shrinks with time, but it is sizable. Also, it is often ignored. Owners of old computers can use substitute equipment with new programs and attachments. The IBM 1401, 360/30, System 3, and, above all, DEC's PDP-8 product line come to mind. A personal computer today can do what every one of them did 15 to 20 years ago—and much more.

At the other end of the product evolution spectrum is the further-out equipment. Most minicomputer manufacturers making any money at all have moved up to the 32-bit machine. Sales for the 16-bit minis are now flat; they have been taken over by the micros. The manufacturers who marketed the 16-bit PCs targeted some markets for them:

- First, as relatively high-performance, small-business machines to do jobs that the minis couldn't possibly do in the past because of cost.
- Second, thanks to their communications capabilities, they can be high-performance workstations in the larger corporations.
- Third, distributed data processing is just offstage.

Technological developments will accelerate the upward trend in applications and alter many of our concepts. This will be particularly true as the 32-BPW micros come into and gain a significant share of the PC market. To appreciate the potential impact, recall that, until 1982, most desktop personal computers were restricted to 64-Kbyte (K = 1024) main memory by the addressing range of their microprocessors. Even among minicomputers few offered more than 512-Kbyte main memory. The plummeting price of random-access memory now allows various 32-bit supermicro computers to offer up to 2-, 4-, and 8-Mbyte (M = 1 million) main memory. Eager to capture the developing markets, microprocessor manufacturers are now boosting high-speed storage.

The cutting edge of technology has this lesson for us: Continuing advances in very large scale circuit integration (VLSI) mean that increasingly complex logic can be integrated on a single chip for packing into a desktop (or, preferably, desk bottom) PC. And that holds great promise for applications.

All things considered, from support software to computing power, there is nothing a mainframe does that a PC and LAN cannot do, except perhaps encryption. This does not affect security in LANs because business environments as a rule don't use encryption. Besides, the industry expects LAN vendors to add encryption boxes to their wares.

American statistics are that only a quarter of all major communications users encrypt voice or data. Most of the encryption is of voice communications; data encryption is still the exception in a business environment, although it is the rule in military and some governmental installations. *Security we can build, but are we able to design the system properly?*

Technical Notes

The advantages of *32-bit* over *16-bit* and in turn over *8-bit* microprocessors lie in speed, capacity, and the ability to directly access larger memory units. The reference is to structural design characteristics: "how many bits" is the microprocessor? For simple computational work, an 8-bit machine is adequate, but for solving sophisticated problems from decision support systems (DSS) to expert systems it would be impossibly slow.

In fact, advanced expert systems need very high power machines. Professor Feigenbaum projects, for artificial intelligence, a need for 10,000 logical inferences per second. The 16-bit IBM 3081 makes roughly 1 logical inference per second; the IBM 3081 supports some 100 logical inferences per second—and that is not enough.

The first generation of workstations used PCs with 8-bit microprocessors. The second featured 16-bit machines, and the third will be dominated by 32-bit machines.

Some personal computers which appeared in about 1983 had both 8- and 16-bit microprocessors to handle programs written for different operating systems, such as CPM and MS DOS. The trend for the best personal workstations is definitely toward 32-bit machines.

CHAPTER 9

Decision Support Systems

The President is a man of great vision—once things are explained to him.

DOUGLAS MacARTHUR

We have been speaking about mental and clerical productivity, and we emphasized that mental productivity applies particularly to the executive's own time. It is, therefore, much more valuable than clerical productivity. As a rule, the value of an employee's time increases with standing in the organization; yet in the first 30 years of computing, the primary focus of analysts and designers was not on the executive suite, but instead on the bottom of the organization.

Nor do executives need a lot of computing power—they just need timely, accurate, exception-oriented information. Their requirement is quite different from that of the lower organization layers for bulky data. In general, within any organization—industrial, financial, or governmental—there are three information layers. The layers are fairly distinct in respect to their content and their presentation of data (Figure 16):

- *Top management* is concerned with strategic issues. Its information environment lacks structure; experimentation with possible outcomes is at a premium; and detail is not necessary, whereas timeliness and accuracy are.

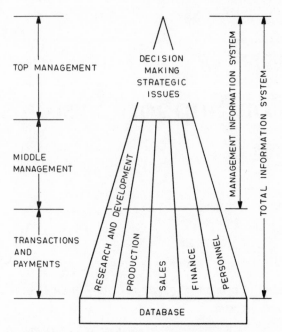

FIGURE 16. The information system pyramid rests on a database foundation and has three main layers.

Senior management decisions are made in the face of uncertainty. As a rule, they involve insufficient information, are interdisciplinary in their nature, deal with the allocation of limited (finite) resources on an organization-wide basis, aim to preserve resources or (usually) increase them, and reflect the dynamic nature of the information environment within which they are made. The construction of the interactive reporting system for senior management must reflect these realities, and so must the database.

- *Middle management* lacks top-management's perspective. Its decisions follow the functional lines of the particular department or division to which it belongs.

Here the goal is allocation and optimization on a divisional basis, the system is semistructured, and the approach taken in study and implementation relies crucially on a continuing program of impact assessment. The effects to be covered should include (1) the opportunity for better control of a given functional organization that can be provided by increased communications speeds and (2) the psychological stresses that can be caused by the need for increased personal work discipline.

- *Lower management* and day-to-day operations have quite different information needs. The aim of a data system at this level is transactions and settlements—essentially the movement of money in and out of the organization.

At this level—which is structured, has established procedures, and is characterized by clerical rather than mental productivity—the objective of computers and communications is different than we have identified for the other two layers. The goal is to improve the efficiency of current operations, which is a different matter than improving the cost/benefit performance of the overall business.

The three layers have many things in common; contingency planning and the ability to prepare for successful interaction with the database are foremost among them. But they do have more in common two-by-two than all three together. In this sense:

- The management information system (MIS) organization addresses itself to the two top layers, and that is true of mathematical models for prediction and experimentation also.

- The lower two layers run along functional lines and feed on a detailed database. The top layer, as we will see, has different requirements.

- Again for the two upper layers, the scheduling of commitments, workloads, costs, and resources available may preclude using the classroom approach to training, which should not be the case with the lower stratum.

Yet because of the rapid advance of technology, an organization, to get its money's worth out of its investment in computers and communications, should be particularly sharp in conceptual training, that is, in changing the mentality of the people expected to use the computer-based tools and the new methods.

Information Systems for Strategic Planning

We said that, at the top-management level, the primary information system (IS) interest should be strategic: forecasting, planning, and controlling the organizational course and focusing on the company image. Experience teaches that there are significant discrepancies between the image a company has of itself and the images perceived by its customers. Those differences can be critical in terms of their future impact.

For example, a firm that feels it is technically superior in an era when cost is becoming the significant competitive factor may find that its image of being *high priced* is more important to its future than its *quality* image. Computers cannot by themselves provide such information, but they may, by integrating data, alert management to the situation.

In general, company image may be assessed in two basic respects: *products* and the *organization* to manage the resources. The key aspects of product are:

- Price, novelty, quality, and reliability
- Management skills and capabilities
- The ability to meet customer requirements

Organization management typically requires:

- Ability to manage change from planning to control
- Personnel quality, including updating personnel skills
- Responsiveness to client demands
- Integrity
- Ability to respond to market forces
- Negotiation skills

Each of these requirements can be reduced to its elements, with the reporting structure common to all. In business and industry, we find something similar in the cost system (Figure 17).

However, analysis into component elements and development of a cost structure call for procedural studies prior to using computer-based

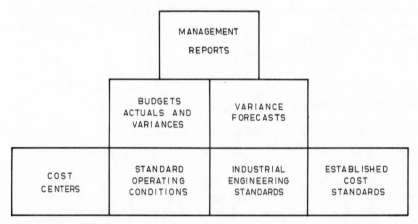

FIGURE 17. A cost system is composed of seven basic elements culminating at the management reporting structure.

tools. To identify the important dimensions of product and organizational image, we must do the proper testing. Test results might, for instance, suggest that the firm has potential problems with the degree to which management and customers are interacting or with the products' market appeal.

Whether we proceed through qualitative evaluation of the kind we have been discussing or quantitative inference from a mass of data available in the database, the process will involve basic disciplines (sciences, mathematics, modeling) and aim to establish the needed grounds for creative projects (engineering, measurement, design, presentation for decision support). This interdependence between the real situation (creative projects) and the idealized (basic disciplines) is shown in Figure 18.

It is important to realize that, as emphasized in the introduction to this chapter, the managerial and operational information requirements are far apart. A study (even a very good study) done to answer the needs of the one will not satisfy the demands of the other and may even be harmful to its interests. Table 15 explains the reasons by using as factors data, applications, volume, and response time.

The role of management-oriented qualitative evaluations should not be underestimated. Some studies unearthed an image that was really surprising to executives: an honest and technically competent organization that lacks marketing aggressiveness. One image study has revealed that a given firm's products were rated high in terms of operating characteristics—performance, reliability, and ease of maintenance—but low in product development effort within stated costs and schedules.

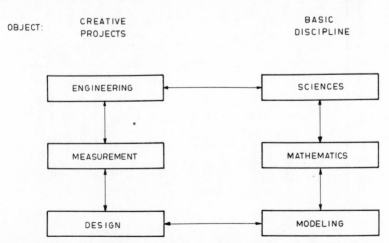

FIGURE 18. The real situation (creative projects) and the idealized basic disciplines are interdependent.

TABLE 15 *Operational and managerial requirements*

Data	Applications	Volume	Response
	Operational		
1. Detailed 2. Volatile 3. Requiring frequent update 4. Current 5. Subject to recovery in case of failure	1. Repetitive 2. Predefined 3. Massive 4. Originally paper-oriented with visualization as a substitute	High	Critical in terms of RT update, but a few seconds delay admissible in reporting; mainly positional
	Managerial		
1. Synthetic 2. Stable 3. Non RT update 4. Historical tendencies, correlations 5. Elaborated data with ample back-up at operational level	1. Nonrepetitive 2. Not predefined—hence modular, flexible 3. Exception reporting 4. Basically visualization; preferably graphs and color	Low	Noncritical in RT update Critical in ■ Immediate response ■ Security protection ■ Graphic presentation ■ Algorithmic support ■ Directional sense

RT = realtime

142

A subsequent *strengths and weaknesses* evaluation identified these major strengths: technical expertise, machine capability, maintenance support, and an international sales force. But it also identified these major weaknesses: a low market share, lack of product standardization, high cost of manufacturing, and a high-price image.

You might wonder what all this has to do with computers. The answer lies in the interactive, timely, and documented reporting to which we have referred. It is unavailable without computer support. Senior management should have easy, user-friendly access to the database in order to evaluate strengths and weaknesses. As we will see later on, this management-oriented database can easily be extracted from the results of the day-to-day operations, formatted, and presented for management decision, provided the right preparatory work has been done. This is one of the main advantages to management of a videotex system.*

When properly presented for management attention, strengths-and-weaknesses reports can play a crucial role in assessing competitive capabilities, revealing opportunities, and providing for risk control. They can support concise statements of the strategic items which are most significant to various client groups or environments and which therefore affect the organization's choices.

This is only one example of why management needs a communications mechanism through which the current situation and future opportunities can be assessed. It reflects the influence of such forces as competitors, the market's drive and potential, the company's own image and its products, and the way the organization itself is structured and operates. Computers and communications will not necessarily make a successful organization out of an unsuccessful one, but lack of action in that direction may inhibit a good one in its struggle for growth and survival.

Meeting Management's Needs

Top management needs a mechanism that constantly brings to the desks of senior executives three crucial questions:

- What is to be done?
- Are we doing it?
- Is the last policy working?

---

* A videotex, or interactive message, system can be public, such as that offered by AT&T and its partners, or private. For the latter part of this decade, private videotex holds a much greater potential than public videotex offers.

In any organization, the chief executive officer needs only a few simple ideas. The CEO should not explain, not elaborate, not excuse. Complexities belong to the middle levels; if they reach the top, they paralyze. And it is equally true that the CEO cannot be exposed to a hundred ideas and then mark time like a centipede.

Top management should never feel that it has solved a problem if all its immediate assistants accept a decision because it's either meaningless or ambiguous. Particularly the CEO's decisions must be:

- Clear and understandable
- Unambiguous
- Able to give direction

If a decision can be misunderstood, it will be! And if a decision is misunderstood, the CEO will get most of what is wanted least, everyone down the line will be overwhelmed with trivialities, and the company will lack direction. Making a decision clear requires skill, practice, and—most important—daring.

Daring decisions can be made when the visibility is good and feedbacks work fast enough to provide for timely corrective action. The latter calls for an information system which covers all basic management functions: planning, marketing, sales, inventories, and manufacturing. The automated administrative duties are the pivot (Figure 19). And we must make the interactivity between the manager and the information

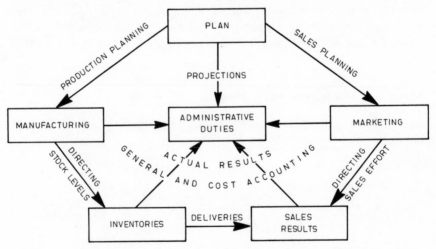

FIGURE 19. An information system must include all basic management functions and respect their interdependence.

more effective by developing *aids* to management decision: an easily understood graphical presentation supported by algorithmic expressions.

As Table 16 outlines, there have been great advances in giving management IS tools it can use effectively. The evolution was made possible by micro- and minicomputer-based systems which, at reasonable cost, effected data processing and database distribution that brought computer power right to the place where the job is done.

The manager must be given hands-on access to business data, which enables the person with the problem to get important information quickly and when needed. The information should be *directional,* rather than positional, and it should rest on an integration of goals between decision makers and information providers.

A decision support system (DSS) should be so designed that it can respond to the information needs of users at each level. It should assure "easy" transition to new systems without upsetting current structures— until they are replaced. And it should assure compatibility of the systems architecture, the communications solutions to be adopted, the computer-based processes, the databases on which these processes operate, and the functional relations which are involved.

To achieve these results within a DSS environment, information systems design must have a goal. Software is important without a doubt, but both computer manufacturers and independent software houses have brought many application packages to the market. Rather than reinvent the wheel, the systems architecture should plan for integrity: error reduction, journaling, and security and protection as they apply to the management level to which the system is addressed.

TABLE 16 *Data processing and database distribution*

Functional level	Original approach	Middle program	Present approach
Top management	No support	Centralized DB (batch)	Inquiry timesharing on mini
Middle management	Centralized DB (batch)	Some inquiry capabilities	Functional DB on dedicated mini
Operations	Centralized DB (batch or online)	Realtime with long telephone lines	Geographically distributed DB on local mini

DB = database

145

From an applications standpoint, a recommended development of a computerized, interactive system for management would:

- Have a time-series-oriented data storage facility
- Accommodate external as well as internal data sources
- Provide for narrative along with the statistical sets of data
- Assure flexibility of response, including spontaneous as well as scheduled types
- Be open to graphics, preferably in color

The DSS should enable the user to communicate directly and quickly with data and evaluate alternatives while making full use of the analytical aids, provide features which allow a decision maker to pose and repose questions considered crucial for decisions, incorporate facilities that make the system easy to use, be adaptable to a changeable environment, and anticipate an evolutionary development cycle.

But as cannot be repeated too often, computers and communications alone will not change our fortunes. We must alter the way we look at our people. In the latter part of this decade and into the 1990s, one of the CEO's most difficult problems will be human obsolescence: We have steadily lost contact with our people in explaining what the future will look like. Now we have to provide this *future vision*—through lifelong learning.

Finally, the support of DSS facilities through computers and communications will be that much more effective if we reorganize our firms for the coming challenges. The company of the future will be based on three basic structures:

1. Projecting
2. Procurement (internal or external)
3. Marketing

We have entered the decade of dehierarchicalization. The user modules of the DSS should emphasize in each of the above three respects decision options and the processes which underlie them. Such modules can act as prototypes of the decision process and thereby, allow quick response and growth in concert with the needs of management. Typically, they will access a database, display information personalized to the decision maker's style (patterned to the environment to be managed), and make possible sets of choices developed to visualize the alternatives to be analyzed for the decision. It is in this sense that interactive videotex should be examined.

Graphics for Management*

Computer graphics have been used for two decades in engineering, architecture, and military applications known as computer-aided design (CAD). Recently, companies have begun to use computer-generated graphs and charts as presentation tools in boardroom settings, and they have also begun to integrate computer graphics into decision making.

The tabular data which has for a long time served (and often annoyed) management can be converted through the computer into graphs. The results are to make the predominant trends more evident and show the direction of the developments which are taking place. Both aid greatly in making decisions.

There have been many successful applications of the conversion of long tables to graphical form. Similar examples can be found in the conversion of printed output to videotex. Management graphs generally present information visually, and they have a powerful impact. Computer graphics channels this same power into a wider range of application areas; they turn tabular data into dynamic visual presentations which, when properly planned, are easy to access and grasp. Since video presentation will be the dominant medium of the future, the color and graphical approaches to man-information interactivity will be fully exploited.

The hardware criteria for good graphics work are resolution and dynamic picture update. If the process works on 8-bit microprocessors, the time necessary to obtain good resolution is relatively long. Indeed, for any kind of modern application, 16- and 32-bit microprocessors should be chosen. Only for data entry is an 8-bit microprocessor acceptable, and there is no real cost difference between the 8- and the 16-bit microprocessor anyway.

The selection of a good graphical system for management involves much more than this basically hardware matter. Yet at any instant, the number of available choices and selections should be small; too many choices create confusion. Some issues are straightforward. Provisions for helping the user have to be built into the system. The user must be offered more information or details upon request. When the system detects erroneous or invalid requests, it must explain to the user how to insert correct information; hence, it must be user-friendly and forgiving.

Aborting the session by stating that something is wrong is not adequate; clearly stated diagnostic messages and illustrative examples must be built in. The user has to have an obvious and ready means of correct-

---

* This is only an introductory discussion. An extended presentation is given in Part 3.

ing or changing inputs. An erase feature should take the user back to the preceding frame. The program should acknowledge each transaction; a feedback to the user is most welcome. The management analyst will be well advised to pay attention to the following:

1. Getting a clear definition of end user functioning
2. Solving the human engineering problems from the start
3. Providing sufficient flexibility for future capabilities to be added
4. Getting the whole system to respond to requirements (For instance, a factory information system will be of no particular value to manufacturing management unless the inventory control capabilities are properly supported.)
5. Looking at response time requirements and doing something about them
6. Examining whether an executive memo pad, the graphic requirements, and so on, are logical extensions of the now-projected system
7. Establishing whether prompting capabilities are necessary
8. Training management in the use of interactive graphics

There is no need to train management in system implementation or engineering; training should be oriented toward the range of services which can be obtained, the capabilities, and the constraints. To follow up on the question "what we can get out of microprocessor-supported graphical facilities," management should be made aware of the advantages but also be informed of the constraints: speed of response, range of applications, and trade-offs. Trade-offs can be decided after the functional requirements are known; they will involve hardware, software, resolution, detail, backup, and system availability. To establish and implement the choices, there should be an alternating consideration of design characteristics and management response. This is definitely an interactive process.

Because technology is continually advancing, training is an integral part of modern financial and industrial life. Graphics offer management new vistas, stimulate the need for better information, and encourage the trend toward more contact with the realities for which a manager is responsible. But end users must also know what to do with the tools we put at their disposal. When new big steps are taken, many time-honored approaches change. Socrates thought the invention of writing "will create forgetfulness in the learners' souls because they will not use their memories."

By training management in technical subjects, we stand to gain better understanding and cooperation. But the question is how much training we can expect. Most managers spend their time with brushfires and don't have enough resources left for strategic planning—and much less for mastering the technical aspects of new graphics systems.

Unfortunately, it cannot be said too often, tools alone are no solution. The manager sitting at an interactive terminal is like the driver behind the wheel: the speed of the car, the curves that can be negotiated without accident, and the security of the system as a whole are up to the driver. The terminal, like the car, must be operated. The goal should definitely be to so educate managers, support staff, and all end users that they can participate in the planning, development, and implementation of a functional, interactive, graphical information system.

The depth of training is a function of the use to which the graphics system will be put and also of the extent of use throughout the organization. If the usage is to be generalized, it is appropriate to elaborate a medium- to long-range plan and set service objectives, budgets, and priorities. The total graphics systems effort should be run like a business: the strategy established, effective communications with the users ensured, and resources utilized at all organizational levels.

Costs must obviously be controlled and made commensurate with results; operations can be streamlined through both procedural and software standardization consistent with the implementation plan. Because graphs are addressed to management for decision making purposes, it is wise to create a high-level management group to involve users, set direction, and review systems projects for overall corporate integration.

It is equally advisable to support operations and decision making down to the level of middle managers, who must often view needed information from four directions: function, business, area, and product. Through procedural realignments, the analysts should strive to improve the interdisciplinary flow of information and create a demand for consistent, flexible, and much more integrated graphics services.

Using Graphics

Among the critical questions for evaluating the interaction between the manager and the computer-stored information we distinguish the following:

- How much prompting?
- How many functions?
- What type of presentation?
- What kind of display?

- How should the communications capabilities be oriented?
- What is the storage availability?
- What are the characteristics of the keypad or other hand-held device?

Undoubtedly, the most important systems query has to do with overall integration; an office information system ranges from board members to secretaries. Typically it should involve all operating departments (through a local network) and all the distributed information systems activities as well. Each of these areas will impose its own prompting, presentation, and display characteristics, but the areas should have in common easy, interactive access. To managers accustomed to spending hours over stacks of computer printouts, graphics come as a welcome relief.

When we look at rows and columns of figures, we have to do the interpretation in our heads; but when we call up charts, we see relations vividly displayed. Moreover, when the analysis is done, the graphs are an effective device for highlighting the key issues for management decision. This, too, has an effect on mental productivity.

A General Motors study found that the use of computer-produced graphs instead of long computer printouts had trimmed to as little as 20 minutes the meetings that had once run longer than 2 hours. At General Mills and Boeing, computers are now converting endless columns of numbers into colorful charts, graphs, and maps that are helping managers spot trends and make decisions more quickly and effectively than ever before.

At Boeing Commercial Airplane, a division of Boeing, charts that once took as long as 2 weeks to develop are presently produced in a few hours. That enables managers:

- To see more up-to-date data and to request new presentations on short notice
- To explore a lot more alternatives

At the Cadillac division of General Motors maps which in the past were drawn up manually could take as long as 2 years to complete. By the time management got them, they were obsolete. Now the data gathering might still take months, but the maps themselves are produced in less than a day.

With graphics, managers can absorb three times as much information in a given amount of time. Computerized graphs can forcefully alert managers to potential problems before the problems get out of hand. The next step in the use of business graphics is for managers to use graphics terminals directly instead of requesting charts from an outside service bureau or in-house data processing staff.

Leading companies plan to install a software package that will enable managers to use the graphics system from any remote terminal in the United States. To be sure, few observers expect senior executives to sit at graphics terminals, but:

- The middle manager can look at twenty representations and then decide which six he wants to present upstairs.
- Top managers will be able to play more what-if games by asking the computer to plot the results of more than one business scenario.

Financial executives can use the computer mapping system to project the variation in revenue that would result from various placements of funds. Similarly, marketing managers can experiment with the assignment of sales personnel.

Yet, computer graphics is still a new tool, and as such it must be used with care. It is in this perspective that the interactive videotex process discussed in Parts 2 and 3 should be seen. In both parts the accent is on preparation; as always, that is the real bottleneck in any information system. Because tables and graphs are framed and presented to the user page by page, it does not mean that the construction of the database should be taken lightly or that little thought should be given to the way the interactive system works. We will turn to these issues in detail in the discussion of the design and editing of graphs.

CHAPTER 10

Betting on Expert Systems

Man is nothing but the strength of his spirit.

MENACHEM BEGIN

Knowledge-based systems provide facilities beyond the decision support system (DSS) capabilities in use since the mid-1970s. They make feasible the creation of *knowledge banks,* which include:

- A methods base
- A methods description language
- Methods specifications
- A growing set of rules

The services supported by a knowledge bank can be employed to assure new system capabilities. Response to queries based on artificial intelligence, consultations, inferences, and the operation of other systems such as robotics depend heavily on the methodologies stored in and updated through a knowledge bank.

These approaches reflect an ever-growing sophistication. They are necessary as the processes we must handle become more complex. Knowledge-dependent solutions are critical in attacking problems related to complex classes of entities. Typically, they are characterized by interactions requiring *expert system* (Esystem) support.

Along this line of reasoning we can see three layers of software made available to management for contributing to the intellectual part of executive and professional work. From top to bottom they are:

1. *Artificial intelligence machines* with reasoning capability including inference and full documentation of the advice given
2. *Expert systems* enriched with knowledge banks, rules, methodology, and nonprocedural method description languages
3. *Decision support systems* answering what-if requests, evaluating alternatives, and presenting a quantitative approach to management

The first Esystems to be designed and implemented were used for medical diagnosis; medicine provides a fertile ground for Esystem development. Engineering has been the next most favored implementation field; within it system optimization and geological applications are specific areas of interest.

In the coming years, Esystems software will make computers even easier to use than with the currently available fourth-generation languages (4GL). Some companies are already working on programs of significant sophistication, such as programs that will be able to remember an individual's habits in using the computer.

Originally designed for mainframes, Esystems have found their way to personal computer (PC) implementation. What is more, they will soon be offered by software publishers. The first commodity-type applications of Esystems will probably be to use rudimentary pattern-recognition techniques in tutorial programs that teach novices how to operate software. The system will adjust the tutorial level after first determining the proficiency of the user running the program.

Indeed, a major drive in Esystem research centers around solving the problem of adjusting to end user working habits and expertise. This is a step forward from the nonprocedural programming languages. As with systems which were originally designed for database management (DBMS) and then used as fourth-generation languages (4GL), Esystems will evolve into very high level programming facilities. They will be fully initiated, projected, manipulated, and maintained by computers. This is the sense of fifth-generation languages (5GL).

EMycin, the language in which Mycin was written, shows the way.* But the most promising developments are the generic processors. At the same time, Esystems represent a convergence of decision support tools toward integrated functioning. Current DSS software will typically reside in the Esystem knowledge bank. It will be automatically upgraded

---

* EMycin stands for Essential Mycin, which is an underpinning of Mycin, the expert system for medical diagnostics. Other Esystem languages are Prolog, Lisp derivatives, and Rosie.

and updated as experience in a certain applications environment accumulates.

Knowledge Banks versus Databases

A knowledge bank is a set of rules stored in the expert system. The now-evolving knowledge banks will be significantly larger than any storage previously attempted or represented in database mapping. Typically, they will consist of *several thousand rules,* and they will steadily expand. Research will concentrate not only on the kernel of the Esystem but also on its facilities, such as processing speed (turnaround), vision, and natural language understanding. This will lead to new computer architectures.

The rules in the knowledge bank will not only be able to produce accurate decisions; they will also document the choices being made. There are, however, challenges to meet:

- Rule extraction is one bottleneck.
- How to manage the rules is yet another challenge.

The crux of Esystem design is making models from perceptions. But Esystem studies can suffer from the problems that plague conventional system design efforts. Inexact programs will be designed if people are inexact when they try to explain what they do and need. Esystems designers have an invaluable tool for managing the inexact nature of typical current work—provided they themselves are exact in what they are doing.

When comparing knowledge banks to databases, we should always remember that methodologies have been available in procedural systems but have not been formalized. They are formalized with the knowledge bank. The process, from the establishment of formalisms to their implementation and policing action, calls for a specific methodology, which itself is part of the knowledge bank. A key question in establishing the methodology is whether it is possible to completely formalize all information:

- Text and data
- Graphics and images
- Edited choice (for input, transport, output)
- Design specifications
- Rules governing the methodology itself

On the basis of those features, Table 17 contrasts a database and a knowledge bank. A knowledge bank might handle the rules it stores through multiple cycling. Interpretation would then require its own rules to govern the flow of control.

Expert systems use the kind of knowledge that a human uses. They can justify their judgments in terms intelligible to users. But how can we define *human intelligence?* It operates on *world knowledge,* the information we acquire through formal education and day-to-day experience. This knowledge ranges (1) from the perception and remembrance of facts to (2) crystallized intelligence and (3) fluid intelligence.

Crystallized intelligence is our ability to use an accumulated body of general information to make judgments and solve problems. It comes into play in understanding and dealing with problems for which there are no clear answers but only better and worse options.

Fluid intelligence is the ability to see and use abstract relations and patterns. With age, the fluid intelligence curve bends downward, but the growth of crystallized intelligence of people who remain logically and physically active can continue well into the eighties. Key factors include:

A. *Staying involved,* as contrasted to withdrawing from life.

B. *Being mentally active*—continuing intellectual interests. This increases intelligence through old age.

C. *Having a flexible personality,* that is, tolerating ambiguity and enjoying new experiences.

People capable of that A, B, C maintain their mental alertness best through old age. But there's hypothesis that Esystems can excel human beings in all three respects. Resting on higher-speed switching circuitry with large storage capacity, Esystems bring all the benefits of computer-based processes to the tasks being executed. That is why *cognitive psychology, complex information processing, and machine intelligence are different views of the same aggregate.*

TABLE 17   Contents of a database and a knowledge bank

Database	Knowledge bank
1. Information elements subject to: • Input • Update • Retrieval	1. Relations between information elements 2. Decision rules 3. Consistency control 4. Access control 5. Propagation actions 6. Dynamic extensibility

Therein lie the reasons why knowledge-based systems provide facilities well beyond those of the decision support systems available since the middle 1970s. Most significantly, as developed above, the facilities provided by a knowledge bank can be employed to assure new system capabilities.

Esystems are specialized. The knowhow-dependent processes are useful for solving problems related to a class of objects. Within this class:

1. Knowledge-based systems make a wide use of methodology and specifications integrated into the components forming the aggregate.

2. Such methodology implies a rigorous discipline that both the machine software and hardware (SW/HW) and the human user should follow.

3. A knowledge-based system acquires a fourth dimension beyond the three already provided by databasing, data communications, and data processing (DB/DC/DP).

Rules attach certain qualifiers to conclusions. This is a dynamic process and, furthermore, Esystem calculations and exploitations may involve probabilistic reasoning. Because the rules must be precise and the inferences to which they lead concrete, successful Esystem development should itself be subject to a rigorous methodology. Successful projects typically:

- Address themselves to small, well-defined fields
- Cover limited domains of knowledge
- Are characterized by a high level of knowhow applied to their development and use

Esystem development is not a lengthy business, however. An advisory system I have in mind involved 6 man-months of computer specialist work and 2 man-months of a professional advisor distributed over a total of about 3 calendar months of development and testing.

Since efforts in that direction have in common a background in methodology, their strength lies in lessons learned. Expert system design starts with working principles and follows a given path. This path involves the convergence of many disciplines to create an artificial intelligence product. Instrumental to that convergence of artificial intelligence and human knowhow is the *emerging understanding of thinking as information processing*. The process involves seven steps:

1. Define the cognitive task.
2. Observe humans performing such a task.

3. Record behavior in protocols.

4. Study protocols to formulate theory of subject behavior.

5. Write programs according to theory.

6. Run a program on same problem(s) while keeping a trace.

7. Compare protocol to trace; evaluate the theory.

Table 18 brings into perspective hardware, software, and knowledge bank features divided into three groups: (1) memory capability, (2) processing power, and (3) interactive characteristics.

Interacting with the Expert System

We have seen that Esystems are characterized by knowledge banks which include methodologies, rules, languages, specifications for methods and rules, and standards. On the basis of the facilities supported by those features, the banks respond to queries in a documented and factual form, make inferences, proceed with extrapolations, and make justifications.

Once fitted into the environment in which they are projected to work, they feed on information, adjust their rules, and develop greater flexibility. The difficulty of an application is related to (1) the quantity and complexity of the requisite knowledge bank and (2) the character of the inferences which are required. These two factors impact on the character of the primitives which must be featured at the Esystem level. An approach to a priori assessment can be based on experimentally determined human information processing characteristics.

Not only should the consulting activity to be accomplished by the Esystem reflect both insight and foresight but the interaction with the Esystem must be flexible yet explicit. When we talk of interaction with the Esystem we must distinguish

1. The interaction of the Esystem with the designer teaching it more rules

2. Commodity offerings to be tuned to a specific environment

3. End user interaction with the specific environment

In *designer communications,* the main problem is the acquisition of knowhow. The best approach is the design of:

- Self-teaching, self-learning systems
- Computer induction of programs from data
- Other forms of reasoning, including concept formation

TABLE 18   A comparison of hardware, software, and knowledge bank features

Hardware	Software	Knowledge bank
Memory capability		
Magnetic disks	Databases	Methodology libraries
Optical disks	Data validity checks	Knowledge-intensive
Controllers	Database management	references
Channels	systems	Learning functionality
	Drivers	State representation of
	Program libraries	processes
	Security locks	
	Updated algorithms	
	Consistent images	
	Downloading capabilities	
Processing power		
Central processing units	Applications programs	Procedural system analysis
Peripheral units	Modules and routines	System design
Means of data flow	Control identification and	Program design
(intelligent channels)	verification	System and program
	Means of program portability	documentation
	Error handling	System and program test
	Recovery and restart	references
	Monitoring and scheduling	Means for device and
	of resources	applications
	Setting of priorities	independence
		Authentication
		Cryptography
Interactive characteristics		
Video display (color,	Cursor	Man-information
graphics, image)	Text editor	communication
Printer	Character strings	Expert system features
Plotter	Case constructs	Inquiries
Graphic tablet	Image file	Menu techniques
Light pen	Graphical presentation	Keyword search
Keyboard	Text, data, graphics, image	Message handling
Functional keys	integration	Presentation technology
Mouse	Electronic mail capabilities	Prompting and help
	Videotex send/receive	Training sequences

Mastery of world-class skill can require the acquisition, storage, and manipulation of more than 30,000 patterns. *Inverse functions* can allow very large question and answer tables to be built. *Inductive inference* will call for fast patterns from examples, with algorithms able to compress the tables into pattern-based decision rules.

Being automated, the Esystem amplifies and/or modifies the knowledge acquired so far: methodology and rules. The precondition is the availability of a machine-executable formal language accepting *concept expressions* and rejecting other inputs as ill-formed. An Esystem language must be (1) pattern-matching, (2) list-processing, (3) object-oriented, (4) recursive, and in accordance with logical inference mechanisms. Such mechanisms must be developed by the designer and grow in a manner transparent to the user.

Machine characteristics should include bit-mapping, window presentation, mouse or other pointing device, good size central and auxiliary memory, and symbolic manipulation. Among the problems to be answered capably we distinguish efficient programming, rule description, effective cross-correlation, and the ability to obtain significant results in the analysis of phenomena and their presentation.

Eventually, knowledge manufacturing will rest on *concept chips*, the equivalent of multilevel circuits. As stated in another connection, very large scale integration (VLSI) promises up to 500,000 components for a few dollars. The basic building blocks will no longer be gates, or multipliers; they will be units capable of speech synthesis, probabilistic reasoning, and so on.

Chip vendors are working now to develop these larger building blocks in an Esystem. The Esystems will become transportable and marketable—they will be comparable to books and software. They will:

1. Represent knowledge in an organized but adaptable manner
2. Support knowledge in terms familiar to end users
3. Employ user-friendly interface functions
4. Exploit the kinds of reasoning which are available

The offerings available at the time of writing can be divided between ready products and language for new Esystem design. Among the latter are EMycin, Rosie, AL/X, Expert, Microexpert, Sage, and Reveal. APL, ADA, Pascal, Basic, and especially Fortran and Cobol, impose an inordinate handling load and contribute nothing to the Esystem program. Currently favored artificial intelligence languages are:

- **Prolog.**   Assures logical inference, pattern matching, declarative approaches.
- **Common Lisp.**   Notations, structured text and data, data and program homogeneity, pattern matching, recursive, list-processing generalization, and dynamic memory allocation.
- **Joint developments.**   Examples are Prolog and Lisp with algoloids.

But the examples which I have given (EMycin et al.) are also well suited for the design of Esystems. In fact, though developed out of a medical diagnostics project, EMycin has been used very successfully as the programming language of projects which range from investment consultation to education.

EMycin and the other specialized Esystem programming languages typically feature:

1. Strategies for incremental rule acquisition
2. Tools for rule acquisition
3. Rule syntax
4. Test and debugging tools
5. Agile consultation facility

EMycin has general applicability and helps build other Esystems, of which Sacon, Puff, and Litho are examples. However, although it has a general knowledge structure, EMycin is not suitable for all applications. Different theories of knowledge representation constitute the basis of the following languages: Age, KRL, KL-One, RLL, OPS-5, Units, FRL, and Omega.

End user interaction makes it advisable that natural language capability, or at least a rich subset of the natural language, is supported. High-resolution graphics, bit-mapping, an agile pointing device, and a keypad (for numeric entries) are musts. Voice input/output is welcome. When the necessary prerequisites are supplied the advantages to be derived from Esystems can be outlined as follows:

- The user has only to formulate logical constructs.
- The user can easily structure acceptable queries.
- The system eliminates unanswerable questions and informs the user accordingly.
- The system prompts and guides.
- The underlying code is very efficient.
- Errors are minimized.
- The knowledge bank grows through self-learning.
- The Esystem justifies the opinion it gives.

The Fifth-Generation Computer

Natural language programming is the approach usually taken in interacting with the Esystem. It enables users to compose English queries for remote databases. The software translates the query into the codes needed to access the database or activate the rules in the databank. Access to data is an integral part of what we can do with the programming language. We also need modeling techniques for dealing with data naturally. Natural language interpreters translate English requests into formal database inquiry commands.

Some offerings act as DBMSs with natural language query facilities and feature fourth-generation application generators. Several components are necessary:

1. Screen and windows

2. Grammar

3. Message builder (and screener of legal set of choices)

4. Interfacing

5. Lexicon

6. Parser

7. Translator

8. Formal query processor

9. Response formulator

10. Report writer and formatter

A most important feature is the understructure: the system must permit the user to easily identify, modify, insert and delete, and generally interact with the natural language programming.

Natural language programming can thus be seen as the front-ending of user interaction with the intelligence residing in the machine. Tools within the broader communications problem are high-resolution graphics, windowing, bit-mapping, agile pointing device, keypad (for numeric entries), and voice input/output.

The user interacts with the intelligence in the machine through menus and pointing devices. The language of the Esystem attempts to reach goals sequentially. For a given goal, it searches to find a clause whose head can be made to match the goal. If the clause is an implication, then it, in turn, attempts to solve the subjects.

The possible result of a goal will be failure or success, plus possible values associated with variables.

- To achieve success for a goal, all the subgoals must be reached.

- If one of the subgoals cannot be reached, the Esystem backtracks and tries to find another clause whose head matches the goal.

- If no untried clauses remain, then failure is returned for the goal.

Important in this search is a split function which differentiates three types of parameters: the empty list, the list whose first element is less than or equal to the pivot, and the list whose first element is greater than the pivot. The Esystem operates by reinvoking a split to partition a list and by using other operators to append the result list.

There are similarities between the new generation of languages and database programming systems: Both have operation on data as their primary goal, with calculation becoming a subsidiary activity. Also, both tend to show *relational* characteristics. A relational technology provides flexible solutions. It is also able to handle unforeseen changes in requirements. This is very important when we need to manage knowledge banks and very large databases. *Dataflow* concepts must be employed.

In a dataflow machine, the processing units do not have to look for data in memory. They address themselves to whatever calculation is necessary when a data packet arrives. Each operation executes automatically once it has sufficient data. The process can be simply represented by data value tokens passing along operation nodes. Graphs can readily be combined by joining their input/output nodes.

Only actual data values, not memory addresses, are passed around the nodes. Hence, calculations cannot interfere with each other by changing the data value in a shared memory cell and thereby creating interlocks or side effects. A dataflow architecture features no central control, so that instructions can execute automatically when all necessary data is available. Graphic terminals can be used to construct dataflow paths to be executed directly as programs by the computers.

Dataflow is one of the architectural approaches to very rapid handling of text, data, and images—both processing and structures. This is a fundamental characteristic of the fifth-generation computer project aimed at designing and producing computer hardware and software for *knowledge engineering* in a wide range of applications:

- Expert systems
- Natural language understanding by machines
- Robotics
- Brain functioning

Several universities and research centers are currently working to decipher the way the human brain works. Unlike digital computers, the brain uses continuous variables rather than discrete binary states. It also operates in a highly parallel rather than a serial manner. Major efforts are also underway to properly identify and eventually bridge the gaps between computers and the brain. Fifth-generation computer projects in Japan and the United States aim to develop processors that function in parallel. At the same time, new theories are applied to software design with the goal of enabling computers to make distinctions on the basis of continuous variables.

The results will impact over a broad range of applications from expert systems and man-machine communications to robotics. If successful, these projects will improve present computing and programming capabilities dramatically. They will permit major innovations in existing technology and enable the new generation of computers to:

1. Support very large knowledge banks
2. Allow very fast associative retrievals
3. Perform logical inference operations as fast as current computers perform arithmetic operations
4. Utilize parallelism in program speed
5. Develop man-machine interfaces that permit significant use of natural speech and images

In addition, developments that are now underway aim to demonstrate that machines can exhibit artificial intelligence. They can think and reason somewhat like humans and understand information conveyed by sight, motion, and speech. By the mid-1990s, both the American and the Japanese leading projects are expected to develop knowledge bank capacity to handle tens of thousands of inference rules and 100 million objects. With fifth-generation computers will come fifth-generation languages typically based on artificial intelligence. Esystems are a paving stone in this development.

Although not yet realized in either hardware or software, such machine architectures are generally viewed as comprising essential features of both computers and communications technology at the end of this century. Biochips and brain augmentation devices may be the basic blocks at that time.

PART 3

How Do We Use Intelligent Workstations

CHAPTER 11

Adapting to the New Technology

Everything must be made as simple as possible.

ALBERT EINSTEIN

Our transition from an agricultural to an industrial society was aided by accumulated experience: more than three centuries were required to transform society in a way that ultimately allowed industrialization to take hold. But the transition to a *knowledge society* in which we are now involved is without precedent. No other nation has developed the wealth and the goods-producing capacity necessary to afford the dedication of more than half its work force to occupations from which no tangible output flows.

If we can understand how an information-rich society can function effectively, we will provide ourselves with a useful model to approach the transition to a postindustrial era. If not, the transformation from the society of today to a more efficient future society will be elusive.

Therefore, as in all major social, financial, and industrial changes, it is the transformation that demands most attention. Transition to new knowledge-intensive goals is more difficult and complex than the changes that were necessary for industrialization. It is, therefore, no surprise that companies unable or unwilling to adapt to the new information technology may lose their competitiveness. This has its counterpart at the national level. Diverting workers from industries with high productivity and effective use of capital into overhead jobs with administrative duties does nothing to increase aggregate economic performance.

The criticism is just as valid for managers as for clerks. There is a trend toward glorifying professionals and managers. However, the results that are achieved by a knowledge worker cannot be measured in terms of tangible products. The only available measure is hours of labor expended, and that's an intangible of rather dubious product value.

Knowledge Workers

The knowledge workers and their staff spend the major portion of their time receiving or transmitting verbal information. Some recent studies suggest that only 8 percent of their time is devoted to "thinking" and another 9 percent to writing. Formal meetings absorb 20 percent or more; two-person conversations on the telephone take an average of 8 percent; travel takes about 10 percent; and the other 45 percent is almost unidentifiable, except to say that it represents various "intraorganizational and extraorganizational" activities. In other words, organization people spend half their time talking among themselves.

All this has evident effects on costs and performance. On the production floor we engage in careful evaluation of measurable product costs, but extraorganizational and interorganizational overhead constitutes so-called undistributed general expenses. Also, these expenses are 7 to 10 times larger than production costs.

This helps explain why many large organizations that employ impressive numbers of knowledge and clerical workers devote an ever-increasing share of their total resources to managing internal overhead. Computers and communications are therefore viewed as the means that might allow us to cope with the limitations in existing administrative systems.

The conversion to the *effective use* of the new tools requires much more than extrapolating from experiences with the automation of standardized clerical tasks. To enhance the effectiveness of knowledge workers, the limitations of existing information structures must be overcome, and that particular task is quite challenging. The unqualified conversion to computers and communications is far from being the proper attack. We must critically examine cost and benefit:

- How can *our* organization profit from the capabilities that technology puts at our disposal?
- Which structural and conceptual changes should we institute to obtain the most from implementation of the new technologies?

- What are the most critical factors to be observed?
- What is a realistic timetable for the introduction of computer-based tools and processes?
- How much training should we provide to convert our human inventory to the new methodology?
- What are the key elements of accurate cost estimating? Of the prediction of benefits?
- Can cost overruns and missed schedules be avoided? How?
- How can the total effort be described? Quantified? Qualified?
- What are the relations between system size, time, and effort? What are the trade-offs?
- What are the cost-estimating risks? How do they vary during the life cycle of the system? Where in the life cycle can cost be reduced? How?

We are beginning to understand how to manage complex information interaction in networks and databases, although we still largely lack the proper institutional setting for knowledge workers in computer-based systems. The technical questions that are raised involve communications protocols, data definitions, access to distributed databases, privacy and security, and so on. Also, there is the very important issue of making sure that the learning levels of all people interacting in the networks are reasonably synchronized.

The earlier we realize that computers and communications are the pivot in the development of our postindustrial society, the better we will be able to define how the larger part of our working population will function. That will eventually lead to a restructuring of the thinking and working methods of professionals, managers, and clerical personnel. Information flows must be managed in a conscious and explicit way to gain a better understanding of the ways in which our information-handling capabilities work and how the underlying powers and costs are allocated.

Although low-cost technological capability is a precondition for greater productivity of knowledge workers, increased understanding of how information can be defined and channeled is the essential challenge. Since knowledge workers devote time to unstructured processing, data-basing, and communications, instead of to well-defined procedural tasks, the difficulty of changing the environment has become evident. Overcoming the difficulty is a vital task. We must apply skill and knowledge to the business of managing change; good intentions are not enough.

Equally important is overcoming resistance to technological and

HOW DO WE USE INTELLIGENT WORKSTATIONS?

structural change. What creates that resistance is fear of the unknown, of being alone, of being lost. There is no reason for fear due to the advance of technology—if we know how to keep abreast of it.

Figure 20 relates plan to structure and structure to efficiency. The plan is needed to provide for orderly progression and to make a realistic allocation of resources feasible. Structure enables us to respond to realities, and efficiency is the best way to assure survival. To set the goals, identify the milestones, and outline the critical steps, we should establish a 5-year plan for the development of our information system.

The 5-Year Plan

We must appreciate the fact that systems changes, particularly those that involve advanced computers and communications capabilities, call for a sequence of changes. On the user's side, the first and most fundamental change is to gain confidence in management by exception. This conceptual change is most important not only because managers must increasingly communicate with machines, but also because machines that tell managers only what's wrong are going to make those managers very nervous.

The current managerial generation has not grown up with video reporting. Things will be different by year 2000 because, with video-games and the domestication of the computer, the new generation will know how user-friendly the system can be. However, at the present time we have a problem to solve, and it can be solved through demonstration and continuing education.

On the implementation side, a most critical change is the institution

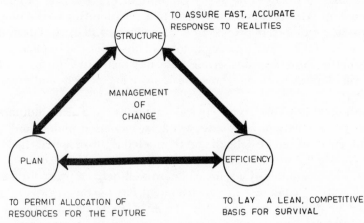

FIGURE 20. The three pillars of the management of change are plan, structure, and efficiency.

of the 5-year plan, to which reference has been made. We must overcome the uncertainties of information systems businesses with plans focused on the long-range profitability of computers and communications. For greater flexibility in preparing the plans, we should investigate several management tools (simulation models among them) which can help us analyze decisions required for long-range strategy.

A cornerstone of the effort is the development of alternative scenarios to determine how sensitive our information systems operation is to changes caused by external conditions. We must also develop the ability to measure the impact of various internal decisions both on the timing of the implementation and on costs.

Long-range planning is nothing new in business. Five-year plans are routinely made for financial, personnel, and product development, market orientation and penetration, and other purposes. What is new is the need to develop 5-year plans for computers and communications resources and to coordinate them with other plans within a given time frame.

What is necessary in order to set up and implement a long-range plan for information systems? We find the following:

- Objectives to be attained
- Resources—physical, logical, and human
- Decisions on how to use our resources
- Priorities in allocating resources
- Procedures to attain objectives
- The proper budget

A clear understanding of the advances in computer and communications technology points in a definite direction: the merger of computers and communications (Figure 21). Within this emerging concept, objectives must be stated in clear terms. For instance:

1. Stop using people as number-grinding machines.
2. Upgrade the information systems capabilities through a step-by-step program.
3. Teach people to challenge the obvious.
4. Be ahead of time—by some years.

The 5-year plan for information systems should provide an infrastructure which is flexible enough to face the requirements for change, yet steady enough to support current operations. We should always be ready not only to adjust the needs to the resources but to adjust

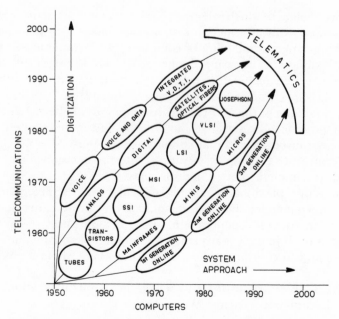

FIGURE 21. The evolution of computers, telecommunications, and semiconductors in the second half of the twentieth century and their merger into telematics, or computers plus communications.

the resources to the needs. We must train our staff and assure that the decision mechanism is open. We must also guarantee that the new technologies do not degrade the security and protection measures which we have enjoyed.

As an example, let's recall that, when records are handwritten, usually only trusted employees have the opportunity to embezzle because only they have access to the books. Computerization means that all the records an embezzler needs for manipulation are accessible at one place: the database. Thus the clerk hired to make routine entries at a terminal could be stealing the place blind by altering accounts payable and receivable, diverting money to a personal account, or juggling payroll data to get checks for phantom workers.

Changes in handwritten books can arouse suspicion, but alterations can often be made in entries stored in computer memory without being detected. Yet computers *can* be programmed to guard against fraud if accounting controls and other safeguards are not ignored. The point is that such controls, once established, are not effective forever. The physical and logical media change within a given time frame, and that should be true of the controls also.

172

A Successful Planning Effort

Prerequisites for a successful 5-year plan for information systems include the able setting of objectives, a steady policy evaluation, the uninterrupted execution of plans, the right decisions on day-to-day issues, and the integration of the short-range time frame within the longer-range perspectives. Every one of these prerequisites requires management attention. Coordination is another reason why steady, well-planned management follow-up is a cornerstone in the successful implementation of a long-range plan in information systems.

To meet the stated prerequisites, we must establish a strategic procedure. The steps are known from other management enterprises:

1. *List possible alternatives* that come to mind and which the advisers advocate (brainstorming).

2. *Briefly examine the alternatives* and choose two or three among them (preliminary analysis).

3. *Provide a detailed examination* of the options retained (logical inference, simulation).

4. *Decide on the course* to follow.

5. Before implementation, *fragment the process* into concrete, coherent, manageable steps (logical organization).

6. *Arrange implementation* so that costly and less reversible decisions appear later on in the process (prerequisites, priorities).

7. *Provide a time schedule* for the implementation action (resources: knowledge, time, money, key physical resources, milestones).

8. *Structure the necessary channels* for the collection and processing of information (feed forward, transmission, feedback).

9. *Review while implementing* (sampling, auditing).

10. *Take corrective action* on plans and their execution.

Trends and tendencies for *the coming years* must be carefully scrutinized to assure that we will be on the right course. Developments which will highlight the 1980s can be put into five categories:

1. **Databases.** Rational database (DB) organization and integration, partitioned and distributed DB, dissociation of the applications programs (AP) from DB access, database management systems (DBMS), rear-end systems, intelligent storage media and logic over data, increases in data volume, and communicating databases

2. **Data communications.** Horizontal networks with thousands of terminals, public service solutions, packet-switching discipline, inter-

networking, satellites and waveguides, wideband communications, substitution of paperwork by online environments, and security, protection, transborder data flow

3. **Decision Support Systems.** Immediate, interactive presentation, user-friendly solutions, mathematics in management (transparent to the end user), experimental capabilities—what-if questions, graphical presentation, color for exceptions, data capture at point of origin

4. **New Media.** Viewdata, integration of telephone and television (voice, image, data), further applications mix (entertainment), personal computers, electronic funds transfer (EFT); generalized use of point of sales (POS); automated teller machines (ATM), home banking, telesoftware, significant investment in the office environment, office automation, a microcomputer on every desk

5. **Basic Principles in Information System (IS) Design.** Layering and functionalization of each layer, single entry, many uses, integrated and then partitioned DB structure, use of data dictionary, ability to bring computer power to the workplace while centralizing software development and maintenance

Computers can help in this approach to information systems development by generating full financial statements for both the operating budget and the strategic plan. A mechanism must be built in to allow the first year of the information systems plan to be used in comparison with the budget and the current budget year to be used as the basis for the next plan. Thus we must cycle through the development of the strategic plan and operating budget and back to the strategic plan again in a way that integrates the plan and the budget naturally.

Since computers and communications are not ends in themselves, the annual profit reconciliation model and report should become a primary feature of the operating budget. A set of reports should be written to show variances between the first year of the strategic plan and the operating-budget year for the financial statements which concern the ongoing implementation of the information system.

This transformation of the computer and communications business from a glamor enterprise to a planned and controlled action of management may generate resistance from people eager to avoid a sense of direction and cost control. As in the case of the ultimate user, there are two ways to face the reaction of the systems specialists:

- *The participatory approach,* or persuasive method. Besides getting the responsible executives involved in the changes in planning and control, education and information programs can be of great help on both sides.

- *The bulldozer approach,* eventually involving intimidation or coercion. In some form or other top management cracks the whip and says: "Get going with this change, or get out."

In the late 1970s, for instance, Lincoln National Life Insurance began planning an ambitious office automation program. Three main objectives were set for this plan, to be achieved by 1984.

- Reduce the use of paper within the company by 90 percent.
- Establish a distributed processing system that ties together all key locations.
- Provide computational capabilities at end user workstations.

The keyword for this program was *participation*—in goal setting and execution. Employee participation was enhanced through a quality commitment program patterned after Japanese *quality circle* involvement, from the rank and file to senior management.

An "automation committee" was instituted to guide the whole effort. A "quality commitment" program was set up, and a new "automated office" department was given line responsibilities for the new systems. "Steering committees" were established with the mission of planning and overseeing departmental implementation of the project.

Quite important, the automation committee was formed by senior management to consider both the direction that data and text processing was to follow and the necessary strategies. In this committee, senior officers and the heads of the operating divisions assumed full responsibility for the management of the information resources within the firm, and they met monthly to review plans requests and progress achieved.

This and other examples document the wisdom that the participatory approach is best tried first. The initial phase is diagnostic: trying to find why some people fight change tooth and nail, make life difficult for management, and erode productivity. The second phase is prescriptive: What tactics can management employ to overcome resistance effectively? Education and explanation are the best guides, and both rest on a return to the fundamentals.

The Communications Activity

In the evolving business environment, a principal issue is *communications.* In origin this is from a Latin word, *communis*; it has to do with achieving commonness. Communications requires not only appropriate technology but also, if not primarily, proper organization approaches, procedural perspectives, and attitudes.

Efficient use of new technology can be assured only by preparation. This is a long and tedious process and is the reason why it is so important to establish and properly implement a 5-year plan. Once this plan is brought to fruition, the resulting system should have another 10 to 15 years of useful life, in spite of the technological advances, if technological trends are forecast accurately.

Reliability engineering suggests that no chain can be stronger than its weakest link, and the weakest link in computers and communications is the human one. The sender must be most careful in phrasing the message so it can be understood without error. Conversely, the party at the destination end must be attuned to message reception. Critical questions at the reception end are: Does the receiver hear it or read it? Understand it? Where does the receiver store it? Is he or she in a position to do something about it? One of the best tests for proper message reception is being able to repeat it without error.

Research data on the communications activity at the sender's end is interesting. The clarity of the message, its structure, the means used for its transmission, and the manner of presentation are factors which play a key role in how well a given message can be understood by the receiver. Sender and receiver interact through the same system. Their performance is closely related to the facilities the system supports, but it is also related to the care with which the system has been set up.

Communications systems are increasingly microprocessor-based. Intelligent, interactive equipment meets with widespread acceptance in banking, business, and industry because of its speed, flexibility, economy, and portability. A microprocessor is a device that follows a plan—provided the plan can be specified precisely as a sequence of steps. The state-of-the-art microprocessor is capable of performing any information-handling task expressed in an algorithmic (hence procedural) manner. By the end of this decade, the algorithmic approach will probably give way to heuristic approaches incorporated first in intelligent machines and then on a chip.

A complete microprocessor design usually involves four components: central processing unit (CPU), memory, interfaces to the peripherals, and channels. The CPU is no longer the central component of a system; it is just one of the subsystems like the memory, the interfaces, and the channels. Still another subsystem is *software,* which can be looked upon as a *deferred hardware design.*

The truly central component of a computers and communications system is *preparation*: the documented study, analysis, and design of the system under development—as well as its subsequent implementation and maintenance. To that must be added the preparation of the human resources who will deal with this system and use it to do their job.

That is why I started this book with a chapter on planning premises—to put emphasis on the adaptation needed to benefit from new technologies before any discussion of technologies themselves.

That is also the reason for including, in the following chapter, a discussion of time management. If we don't learn first of all to manage our time in an efficient manner, the modern tools at our disposal will be of little use to us. It is one of a manager's responsibilities to maximize the effectiveness of the resources under his or her direct control. This is true of money, of knowledge, of time, and of the means technology makes available to us.

Technical Notes

Problem solving can be algorithmic or heuristic; the differences are primarily a choice between procedural and nonprocedural approaches. An *algorithm* is a step-by-step procedure leading from an initial condition to a sought-after end. From that no deviation is possible. In contrast, the *heuristic* procedure is to use trial and error guided by feedback. It is exploratory, although this too rests on rules and principles; it advances learning; and it is creative rather than mechanical and repetitive.

Originally, as we have seen, computers worked only algorithmically: everything the computer was to do had to be carefully specified in the program. That suited the original computer uses and, incidentally, the clerical level of application. In contrast, the expert systems discussed in Chapter 7 require a totally different kind of program based on rules and principles reflected in managerial and professional thinking, which is often heuristic.

CHAPTER 12

Training Management in Computers and Communications

If you plan for one year, plant rice.
If you plan for ten years, plant trees.
If you plan for a hundred years, educate men.

CHINESE PROVERB

The successful implementation of computers and communications is a complex job requiring a well-planned, concentrated, multifaceted effort. Without it, the investment will earn no return. Education is more than part of it; education is its cornerstone. Computers and software, even the most sophisticated, are worth practically nothing without the proper training of the personnel who use them. Lifelong learning should include all levels from top management to first-line supervision and clerical help.

Training is needed to build a common foundation of knowledge among users. The users must become properly acquainted not only with the tools of the new environment but also with the concept of system integration and the new interactivity with their superiors, subordinates, and peers. Training must begin at the most basic level. Users will encounter difficulty translating their computing demands into suit-

179

able information form. They must also learn to organize their logic so they can follow and profit from system capabilities.

Moreover, training must be designed and developed by defining the courses and their sequence, seeing to it that the courses build on each other, and assuring that users don't leave a course without learning some things that help them in their daily work. And since end users have a limited amount of time for training, the curriculum should be organized into short modules.

The NCR Experience

Along that line of reasoning, NCR in the United States organized a seminar for its board of directors. In it participated twelve executives: six per class with one teacher and two assistants. The seminar was on the personal computer (PC) as intelligent workstation (WS). An original approach was to present each participant with a PC packed in its cardboard box to simulate the situation in which the user starts with the purchase of the machine. The same procedure was followed with the modem and the software.

The program can be outlined as follows:

1. There was *no* discussion about the computer and its inner workings—whether hard- or software (HW, SW).
2. Presentation was limited to what was visible: video, buttons (power on, etc.), keyboard, floppy disks, printer, and modem.
3. A particular effort was made to overcome the resistance of some people to touching the keyboard.

The instructor took time to familiarize the participants with their machines. Playing games provided a good basis for learning the keyboard. The approach taken was not to say "Enter DIR" but "Type D, I, and R, and then press the return key."

4. Teaching included how to handle the machine. The instructor explained disk content, insertion, and storage.

Explanations covered disk protection: not using ballpoint to write labels, keeping magnets away from disks, not flexing the disk, and not touching any unprotected surfaces. The trainees were also shown how to put paper in the printer.

5. Explanations covered basic functions such as how to create a backup copy of the software.

The participants were patiently led to understand that MS-DOS provides a menu, in the beginning, on how to make backups and how to use the menu effectively. The same unhurried approach was taken to use of the directory for file lookup.

6. The first application was spreadsheet, with Multiplan.

This started with an explanation of how to open a file, how to make a simple model, and how to handle a floppy disk with data, which was given the participant. The instructor demonstrated the replication functions and taught how to use the help screen. *The participants learned by doing.* Applications included budget evaluation, stock and bond inventory, and stock analysis.

7. The same procedure was repeated with WordStar for word processing.

8. A videotex experience was included by making a connection with CompuServe to access databases.

Participants were taught how to dial a network and then a database, how to use passwords, and how to employ preloaded function keys with the passwords needed to reach the database. Stock-exchange-type applications were selected.

9. The communications experience was broadened to include the handling of protocols.

Different types of data communications connection were demonstrated, and criteria for selection in the event of alternatives were given.

At the completion of the course, the members of the board were able to handle their PCs both in a stand-alone and in an online mode. They had lost their fear of the computer and had started to acquire applications experience.

Practice at United Technologies

The United Technologies 3-day program of hands-on experience for managers highlights the practical way to work with the PC. Lecturing takes only 10 minutes; the rest of the time is given to work on the computer. PC software and hardware (particularly keyboard commands) are explained on the first morning. Also explained are:

- How to use the documentation
- How to load the disk operating system (DOS)
- How to load other software

The afternoon is devoted to practical examples with spreadsheet implementation:

- Salary planning
- Budget comparison
- Sales forecasting

On the second day, the morning work concentrates on management graphics created on the PC by each participant. The afternoon is devoted to word processing software and personal scheduling routines.

The morning of the third day is devoted to communications protocols and software availability with practice in data communications:

- Sending and receiving messages
- Electronic mail
- Connection to the company's own resources

The afternoon work centers on communicating with public databases. The Dow Jones database is the practical example.

Throughout the program, the instructor communicates through a PC and a local area network (LAN). The participants are taught interactively how to use their new skills. They then develop *their own personal computing* plans.

Seventy-five percent of the senior managers who participate in the course take their PCs home and work 1 to 1½ hours every evening to become proficient.

Computer Literacy Training at the Mellon Bank

Mellon Bank of Pittsburgh is the twelfth largest American bank in terms of assets. In 1983 it began a program designed to make all of its employees, from the newest clerk to the chairman of the board, computer-literate. Its training program included:

- Instruction in the fundamentals of computer operation
- The use of personal computers
- The use of inquiry/response languages

In taking that clear-eyed management initiative, Mellon was the first major U.S. corporation of its kind to involve employees at all levels. Computer literacy training is part of a larger program that includes evaluation and selection of professional workstations to be installed in the offices of all members of the bank's middle and upper management.

At the conclusion of a 6-month testing and evaluation period, during which the proposed professional workstations of at least five major micro-computer and office automation system vendors were examined, Mellon Bank expected to issue an initial purchase order in excess of $40 million for the new management tools. Subsequent orders for units at its more than 300 correspondent banks could bring the total value of the order to more than $100 million.

The objective of that investment was to increase the number of people in the bank utilizing computers in their day-to-day activities from 30 percent (most of whom are branch tellers) to 70 percent within 2 years. Both of these innovative programs were mandated by the bank's chairman of the board, J. David Barnes, who dubbed 1983 "the year of technology at Mellon Bank."

Actually, emphasis on the use of advanced technology, particularly computer technology, had been a hallmark of Mellon Bank for some 30 years. Located midway between New York and Chicago, management decided early in the 1950s that the only way the bank could compete with the big banks in those money market centers would be through what then-chairman, John Meyer, called *innovative automation.*

A Proposed Program for Training Senior Management

Many more examples of financial and industrial organizations in the process of training their senior management to operate in a computers and communications environment could be cited, but the two given provide a good background on which to build a program.

The objective of this program is to outline a 3-day suggested schedule of *natal courseware** able to provide direct management hands-on experience.

First Day

1. Workstation program
   Processing machines
   Authorized database access
   Communications
   Time management

---

* A term recently coined in the United States to identify beginning courses in the new technologies—tuned to senior management.

2. Office automation concept
   Software, hardware, and documentation
   Floppy disk with data
   Using the machine

3. Spreadsheet experience
   - Salary planning
   - Loan management
   - Current account transactions
   - Personal treasury
   - Investment accounting
   - Budgeting and control
   - Development forecasts

Second Day

1. Prompts, help screens, and how to get them

2. Graphics
   - Introduction to management graphics and decision tools
   - Yesterday's exercises—from tabular to graphics

3. Word processing
   Electronic mail (Email)
   Calendar services

Third Day

1. Networks
   Communications protocols
   Local area networks
   Applying Email
   Client communication

2. Database access
   Authentication and authorization
   Accessing the company's own database
   Accessing public databases

3. What to do in time out; software failures; hardware failures

4. Reactions, wishes, and recommendations

Retraining the Systems Specialist

The objective of this proposal is educational effort in computers and communications at the senior management level, but beyond any doubt a program—more detailed in its contents—must be developed for the computer specialists. The half-life of technical specialization in this field now stands at the 3 years level. As a minimum, a technical training program should include the following subjects:

1. Nature of the PC as a workstation machine
2. Assured hand-holding procedures for the end user
3. Logical structure of the database
4. Microfile supports (physical and logical)
5. Communications facilities and protocols
6. Local and long-haul network
7. Available software for databasing, data communications, and data processing
8. Fourth-generation languages
9. Inventory of commands and interfaces at the end user level
10. Implementation steps for a smooth transition
11. Solutions with software and hardware failures; self-maintenance
12. Fallback procedures, recovery, restart, self-help

Since past solutions with mainframes were two degrees remote from the end user and minis one degree remote, it is important to teach the system specialist how, with workstations, remoteness has been replaced by full visibility. It is just as important to imprint the notion that end user systems tend to evolve through many versions.

Such development is difficult for most mature system specialists to comprehend, because it means a different world than the one in which they lived until recently. Also difficult for them to comprehend is that system upkeep can be handled through iterative development of different system versions rather than by reliance on the old heavy maintenance. With the workstation, the emphasis changes from "What do we want to do with the computer?" to "What data do we want?"

End user computing can, however, be greatly facilitated by fourth-generation software tools if those tools are understood and properly used. At the same time, fourth-generation languages impose an interactive design as well as a flexible architecture. These two observations are the key to defining a development methodology for end users.

- The first point is that, rather than be preoccupied with data structures, the developer should understand the language's underlying data design assumptions and fit requirements into that design.

- The second point is that, rather than design a given architecture for a fourth-generation language, the objective should be to fit the development effort to the technical architecture provided by the language.

The systems specialist should be taught that very high level language tools are fundamentally different from previous software tools. The pillars on which they rest are two in number: *a facility to describe data outside the processes that use the data* and *the generation of procedural logic based on nonprocedural descriptions.*

Fourth-generation languages have often been characterized as *user level* because they provide a means of describing data externally. What is not often appreciated is that this facility can be ably used by a computer specialist to define initial detailed data descriptions that the user can then access in a variety of ways.

Fourth-generation languages also provide large productivity gains when development conforms to the design assumptions of the product. But they can also end in productivity disasters when the data and architectural assumptions are ignored or misunderstood by the developers. A basic point is that program generators are built around an assumed data structure, and it is essential to understand that structure. Unless the underlying characteristics are understood, they will be violated and the tool will be made counterproductive.

For instance, in a data structure methodology, the database design is driven by how the user will employ the system. In end user environments, these functional requirements are not available before the system is designed; instead they evolve with the system.

Furthermore, technical architecture and system design derive from the information design (text, data, image, voice), which develops as the project moves on. The end user data store is maintained by an information delivery system and, for example, spreadsheet handlers assume that the application requirements can be mapped into a matrix structure.

In conclusion, the basic nature of systems development changes in end user computing and very high level language environments. This is a key point which must filter through the system specialist's store of knowledge. Until it does, the development effort will supply only a small fraction of what it could supply.

CHAPTER 13

Integrated Software and Fourth-Generation Languages

Men will do the rational thing, but only after exploring all other alternatives.

JOHN MAYNARD KEYNES

Integrated software (Isoft) is a single package that combines the functions of several separate applications. It lets the user transfer data easily among the different programs and eliminates much reentry. The user need learn only a single set of commands for the different applications. The number of routines available varies from package to package, and it has an evident impact on central and auxiliary memory requirements.

As an example, the CA-Executive requires at least 256 Kbytes of main memory, and the programs work best with 512 Kbytes. The package comprises eight integrated programs:

1. *CA-Link* ties a personal computer (PC) to a mainframe or other PC running the same package. This communications approach permits downloading and uploading data, as well as emulating a 3270 terminal.

2. *CA-DBMS* is a relational database management system that includes a report writer.

3. *CA-Calc* is an electronic spreadsheet.

4. *CA-Writer* is a word-processing package, including spelling and electronic mail (Email).

5. *CA-Edit* is a full-screen text editor that lets users create and edit files and programs.

6. *CA-Form* is a forms generator.

7. *CA-Graph* generates bar and pie charts and line graphs and handles composite reports.

8. *CA-Tutor* is an online tutorial program.

Each of these components makes use of a window manager, and commands are entered through a keyboard or mouse.

This example demonstrates that an integrated software product performs a variety of functions, though the most common types will have a database management system (DBMS), a spreadsheet program, and a routine to produce business graphics. Isoft also allows the user to perform word processing and line management and to combine information capabilities to produce final reports whether on softcopy or hardcopy.

Note the emphasis on communications. Communications systems are becoming more capable of performing complex tasks, usually faster and more efficiently. There are communications products with a variety of features to fill the needs of different kinds of users, and it is important that Isoft supports features that make it possible for the PC to operate unattended and communicate with other computers.

Component Parts of Integrated Software

Component parts of integrated software can be complete procedures, particularly if they serve other components—which, for instance, is the role of the database management system (DBMS). The database management module of an integrated software offering, Aura, is capable of executing report, sort, elect, edit, and index functions through a menu-driven, fill-in-the-blank user interface. Screens, reports, and criteria for a sort and select function can be quickly established. Data from that module can be included in spreadsheets, graphs, or word processing documents.

With integrated software, the high ground is kept by a DBMS to which attach other packages such as spreadsheets, graphics, word processing (WP), and various calculation routines (Figure 22). We have seen some examples in the introduction to this chapter. The main purpose of a DBMS is to organize and structure data to access and manipu-

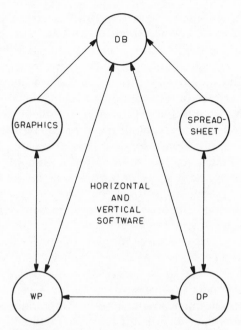

FIGURE 22. With integrated software, the high ground is kept by a DBMS to which attach other packages such as spreadsheets, graphics, WP, and various calculation routines.

late in any way the user chooses. Database software is usually sophisticated and versatile.

Document-handling routines are designed to replace office filing cabinets, and they have a structure similar to that of the DBMS. The primary unit of a database is a *file.* Low-function databases contain only one file per floppy disk; high-function databases have large numbers of files.

A mailing list, for instance, is a *low-function database.* The user can sort data within the database in a limited number of ways, usually by name, address, and the like. *Medium-function databases* are capable of holding more than 10,000 records and feature multifile operations. They can sort data in each record by more than one field type, while allowing the user to create a format for entering and retrieving data. *High-function databases* have all the features of lower-function databases, plus characteristics that permit the user to sort, enter, print, and manipulate in ways not possible with lower-function databases. They make it feasible to attach records from one file to another file while leaving the first file in its original form.

Furthermore, DBMSs embedded in Isoft, as well as the self-standing ones, have "extras" that make them more appealing. For instance, a larger variety of field definitions can be available and the user can produce forms to exact specifications and compare totals, subtotals, averages, maxima, and minima. To protect the data, it may be possible to assign passwords to the fields. Another add-on is the ability to interface with other programs and thus create more complete packages.

Isoft is horizontal software. Some products can be attached to vertical packages, that is, applications programs. Examples are planning, investing, and financial management. Even better, such applications routines are written by using the Isoft as a programming language.

Appointment-scheduling software can provide capabilities useful in accessing or entering schedules about appointments. That eliminates the need for appointment books and confusing calendar changes. It also offers quick access to a large number of entries by managers who are permitted to access other people's schedules. The software sees to it that appointments are so organized that the user can access them quickly. It also permits the user to search for a certain appointment or to enter an appointment where no other appointment exists.

The spreadsheet permits what-if experimentation as well as summarizing available information and providing meaningful support. This will, for instance, aid an investor in following market trends, analyzing favorable investments, calculating the rate of return, handling different currencies, and so on.

Word processing routines are designed to create, edit, and print documents, which may be letters, lists, memos, legal paper, or other kinds of text. To create a document on the PC through WP software, the user follows steps similar to those with a physical word processor. He or she can start by setting tabs, margins, and line spacing and can do so by choosing from a menu. User-definable defaults speed up formatting by numbering or naming each specific document. Isoft may allow use of different formats throughout a document. Creating and saving a document on floppy disks permits the user to return and make changes without having to retype the whole document. Isoft also provides insert, delete, and search and replace functions.

Printing occurs when the user wants it to occur—and with options. During the development of the text, a spelling checker that contains its own dictionary is used to correct spelling. Some offerings permit the user to add what is in effect a supplementary dictionary of frequently used names or special words. Others even call attention to a word typed twice in a row.

A mailing list program is often a coordinate package with some Isoft. The user types a list of records containing names, addresses, or other random information in the document and then a letter or form, containing all portions of the document that do not change from one use to the next. The mailing program prints out one of these documents for each record on the list and inserts the random information where it belongs in the document. Operation does vary from one product to another, however.

Graphics software helps users create a variety of charts to display and/or print. Pie, bar, and line charts are examples. They are two-dimensional, but histograms may also be supported in a three-dimensional form. Prompts help the user create his own designs.

Open and Closed Architectures

The functions described in the preceding sections coexist under the same roof, but there is no unique way for combining the programs concerned. Two main lines toward reaching a software aggregate can be distinguished (Figure 23). One is *a loose association of programs* in which:

1. Independent applications share a common data format. They cannot go in and out of it realtime.
2. Shell programs* provide common menus and data translation among independent off-the-shelf applications.
3. The effect is to support a multifunctional applications environment with the same format.

This is an *open Isoft architecture*. We can add to and subtract from it. It is flexible but penalizing.

The other way toward an aggregate is to adopt a *multifunctional fully integrated* operating environment. This is a *closed Isoft architecture*. It is very efficient, but we cannot easily add new applications. Lotus 1-2-3, Supercalc 3, Symphony, and Aura, cited in the preceding section, are closed architectures. In the Aura case, the Isoft module permits users to create and link together many spreadsheets limited only by the disk capacity of the PC. It can also include information from the database manager, and its results can be graphed or incorporated in word processing documents.

More than fifty functions are offered, including statistical, financial, mathematical, and text operations. Among supported features can be distinguished thirteen-digit precision, full work screen prompts, variable field width, field protection, copy-and-move operations on field blocks,

---

* Window management multitasking like the commodity offering, for example.

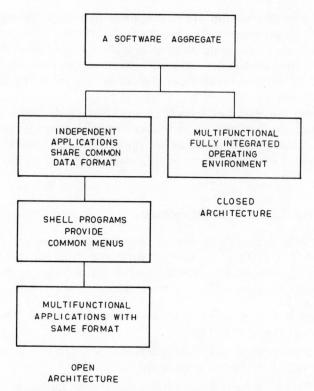

FIGURE 23. Two main lines toward reaching a software aggregate can be distinguished.

help screens, user error messages, worksheet time stamp, horizontal and vertical scrolling, recalculate on/off control, and more.

The word processing module can edit several files concurrently and perform text block operations that also allow moves between documents. It features unlimited document length, help screens, and ruler operations that include justification, headers and footers, and printer control.

This Isoft offering can include information from the database, spreadsheet, or graphics components. It allows graphics command subsets to be used in the spreadsheet as a means of producing graphs quickly and easily. Working with the spreadsheet, a user can set database search and select criteria, choose the type of chart wanted, automatically or manually set chart axes and other parameters—all through menu prompts. Password protection precludes unauthorized access to these operations.

The graphics module offers free-draw graphics as well as the ability to dynamically and automatically alter prepared graphics. With these capabilities, changes in database or spreadsheet elements can be reflected in revised graphs. Graphs can be included in word processing documents.

The application components are fully menu-driven, but there is a menu bypass facility that makes shortcuts possible as users gain experience. These examples of functionality are spreading through the industry in an unprecedented thrust in packaged software. Isoft has become the aggregate of the seven basic horizontal software classes which have emerged so far:

1. Spreadsheet calculators

2. Word processing

3. Business graphics

4. Electronic mail

5. Time management

6. Text and data communications

7. Database managers

In vertical software offerings the most sought for package is accounting. But the integrated software itself is evolving. Lotus 1–2–3 has been the most successful of the Isoft offerings, yet within a year and a half from its introduction to the market it was surpassed by Symphony, another product of the same vendor. Table 19 compares the functioning of Lotus 1–2–3 and Symphony.

TABLE 19   First and second generations of integrated software

Supported functions	Lotus 1–2–3	Symphony
Database	Original design	Improved design
Spreadsheet	Original design	Enlarged design
Graphics	Five graph types	Eight graph types
Word processing	—	Yes (with edit, word wrap, insert/ delete, erase, copy, move, search and replace, substrings, headers)
Windows	—	Yes. Overlapping options, window on top is the active one
Communications	—	Yes. File transmission, log-on to prestore, remote databases, suspend data communications session, analyze data

A Stream of Enhancements

With Symphony, two of the three parts of Lotus 1–2–3 have been enhanced: The spreadsheet is larger, and there are now eight graph types instead of five. The database is completely rewritten. But the most important features in Symphony—the word processing and communications systems—are new, and so are the windowing facility and the open-ended nature of the product.

Symphony includes not only financial management and graphics but also word processing and a facility for transmitting and receiving data over telephone lines. Thus it appears to be a significant improvement in integrated software that combines many of the most popular applications for a personal computer. For instance, stock data can be retrieved by telephone and analyzed through a spreadsheet, which enables users to manipulate long rows of interrelated figures for financial projections. The results could then be put instantly into a letter or a report, along with charts to further highlight a trend.

The word processing part includes such standard features as justification, automatic word-wrap, insert, delete, erase, copy, move, and search and replace. The screen displays lines and character numbers at all times to indicate the position of the cursor.

Format lines can be added to the text to easily obtain automatic indenting of subsections, single-spaced paragraphs in double-spaced text, and so on. Format lines can be edited to change the position of margins and tab stops. Printing options include single-, double-, or triple-spaced lines, underlined or boldfaced characters, subscript, superscript, and headers and footers with automatic page numbers and dates.

The communications system, the other completely new module in Symphony, is asynchronous and offers full terminal emulation, automatic dial-up and log-on to remote databases, easy capture of data and immediate user access to captured data, point-to-point transfer of any file, and full user control of all terminal parameters.

Windows split the screen into segments; they allow a user to see a letter, a spreadsheet, and a graph at the same time. The user can choose among them by pressing a key. Combined with the interactive power of the Symphony window management system, the communications module enables the user to instantly suspend a communications session, analyze the captured data in a spreadsheet, and immediately return to the communications mode. The user can prestore complete communications settings to greatly simplify the process of logging on to remote databases. The communications package uses a file transmission protocol.

Other Isoft offerings include Query by VisiOn. Start/stop and binary synchronous communication (BSC) protocols become commonplace, and the DBMS facilities can be used as a fourth-generation programming language.

About two-thirds of all U.S. companies that bought business micro-computers in 1983 also bought Isoft for making complex financial pro-jections and displaying the results instantly in computer-generated pie charts, bar charts, and other graphic displays. As experience with hori-zontal software products accumulates, users tend to differentiate the offered services in terms of sophistication, and vendors are quick to respond. There is, for example, a subtle difference between charting and graphics:

Charting refers to simple bar, pie charts, and histograms—converting spreadsheets and tabular formats.

Graphics includes icons, multiple windows, and editing of charts.

In the word processing offering there is a need for a *WP style sheet* to help edit along preferences (parameters) and, later on, to provide stepping-stone pagination. Similarly, users would like to see *calendar management* included in integrated software to identify who has the right to call meetings, change calendars, authorize changes, and update all calendars of communicating workstations.

The third generation of integrated software will include:

1. *Creation of system commands* (shells) to make all links (and other sup-ported functions) fully transparent to the user
2. *Encryption* capability (first SW through password, ;IS then SW/HW solutions)
3. *Integration links:* WP to Email; calendar to Email, etc.
4. *Voice editing* based on voice data types (digital encoding) and playback capabilities
5. *Project management* incorporating automatic reporting and plan versus actual, update, PERT presentation
6. *Budgetary control* capability: handling budgets, receiving financial re-ports, and producing highlights, charts, and exception items
7. *Expert systems:* implementing a knowledge bank (rules), presenting conversational reports, and justifying the suggested course of action

The issue to concentrate on is *added value.* That is what the customer wants.

Fourth-Generation Languages

Spreadsheets are an example of fourth-generation languages (4GL). DBMS programming is another example; it ranges from simple query capabilities to relational databases. Still other examples of 4GL are precompilers and shells. The expert systems discussed in Chapter 10 are the beginning of a fifth generation of programming languages. The importance of 4GL rests on three foundations:

1. They make end user programming feasible.
2. They greatly increase professional programmer productivity.
3. They make continuity in software investments feasible, at a very high level.

Hardware products come, go, and are replaced, but applications stay. Therefore, the language is a *strategic* consideration. In a mid-1984 meeting at the Santa Teresa laboratories, an IBM representative mentioned that the corporation used to spend much time and money in labor-hours to write customer programs. Not anymore. Computer-based 4GL tools make it unnecessary. As a result, more time is available for marketing. Fourth-generation languages mean significant simplification in the programming procedures. No previous software development has provided this capability, yet we could have learned a significant lesson from the automobile industry.

In the coming years, *user-driven* computing will be one of the major fields of office automation. It is expected that:

- User-driven computing will reach over 65 percent of the total instructions per second available.
- User-oriented databases will become an integral part of the working environment.

For integrity, security, and cost reasons the appropriate tools have to be carefully customized to the user's requirements. They must also be imbedded in a total information management concept. The parallel is automotive: Henry Ford not only created an industrial mass production line but also simplified the controls of his Model T so that most people could drive it. The computer industry can have computers that most people can program through 4GL and microelectronics.

As far as user involvement is concerned, we can talk of computer programming without professional programmers. That is the most important revolution in computing since the invention of the transistor.

People and machines have very different needs in regard to structure of work. Machine work must be procedural—broken into the smallest parts with little variation. Unlike machines, people prefer to have more challenging and interesting work. People who want to live interesting lives welcome variation. It gives them the opportunity to learn new skills and to avoid repetitive tasks. Skilled persons like to be in control of what they do; they like to make decisions and share in the responsibility for the end product.

Yet, for reasons fairly difficult to explain, computer experts, in response to machine rather than human limitations, have been oriented toward the now obsolete concepts and methods of doing the programming work. Cobol, Fortran, and PL/1 have been their Bible. This has led to boring, repetitive jobs and very low professional productivity.

Fourth-generation languages address themselves not only to the end user but also to the professional programmer/analyst. With 4GL an analyst can obtain results faster than he could write specifications for a programmer. The analyst can also work hand in hand with the user to create what the user asks for and refine it through prototyping.

A 4GL is of great assistance in creating a prototype of the application—a version of the real program not optimized in terms of machine time. It is not the old "feasibility study" on which the computer professional has spent part of his life for no well-defined reason for over nearly 30 years. IBM surveyed people who had been successful in getting the programs they wanted and found that 80 percent of the desired characteristics were *not* in initial releases. Here is where prototyping can be of great help.

There is in this respect another vital reference to Bankers Trust experience. In a critical evaluation it was found that, in 80 percent of ongoing data processing projects, the usefulness was not there: competitors had leaped ahead; the market needs had changed; delays had made certain computer projects nearly unnecessary. This is typical of what happens every day in business and industry. The major merit of Bankers Trust is that not only was it able to carry out a factual and documented audit; it was also able to take corrective action. Others don't do that.

The major advantages offered by 4GL are:

- Flexibility
- Low-cost maintainability
- The possibility of reshaping the application with minor effort

Fourth-generation languages are based on the successful subcomponents of third-generation (high-level) language architectures such as database management system, data dictionary, query and reporting facility, data communications routines, and screen formatting. These components are field-proven and have been integrated with hardware developments.

By providing a new type of standard software, 4GLs greatly reduce any migration problems, including the migration of existing data. After the prototyping is done, they offer the tools for optimization—the whole process being accomplished at 1500 to 6000 percent improvement in coding productivity over Cobol.

A fourth-generation language formalizes the relations, manages the information elements, and proceeds with computation and response. As stated, its structure and content can consist of spreadsheet, DBMS, and macrocommands. In user terms, it:

- Provides computer assistance
- Improves productivity
- Obliges the user to work in a structured manner

The DBMS component assures storage management, retrieval and update, diversified text and data research, database security, personalized format and structure, full-screen editing, and report-writing capability. It leads to calculating functions.

Six key points can be outlined with a fourth-generation language. A successful 4GL:

1. Produces applications programming at least an order of magnitude faster than high-level language after all time spent on user interaction, coding, documenting, testing, and implementing has been considered

2. Employs a syntax which is typically nonprocedural

3. Removes and automates the repetitive detail work in query, reporting, et al.

4. Acts as control language with system commands and integrates instructions written in a high-level language*

5. Can be learned in three days or less

6. Can be understood by both the end user and systems specialist

Add-on functions include screen support, data dictionary, transactional, message, and file exchange, privacy and security, communicating database characteristics, and environmental recovery. Later on in this decade, fourth-generation language will take most of the steam out of applications packages, but today such packages still have their reasons for being.

---

* My advice is to use C or Pascal, not Fortran or PL/1, and never Cobol.

Finally, because they are portable and produce a code which is (in most cases) device-independent, 4GLs permit an open vendor policy based on commodity operating systems. The operating system becomes the common ground on which an organization can standardize. The type of machine behind it is not significant.

CHAPTER 14

Visual Thinking

Each problem solved introduces a new unsolved problem.

POPULAR WISDOM

Menus, windows, icons, mice, bit-map displays. These are some of the elements of the new generation of user-oriented software and hardware. Their presence is changing the way users and computers communicate. The objective of the new functionality being developed is effective user interface design. It should be kept foremost when we talk of the importance of graphics, how user testing is done, software development, and the key elements now available to help in the communication between the user and the information available in the computer.

Most of the new offerings support multiple windowing and overlays on the primary page. These are more meaningful with the pop-up menu approach. Furthermore, 32-bit machines support changes in graphical presentation which can be made through icon selection. The user can switch from a histogram, to a pie chart, to a three-dimensional business graph. Given the power of the microprocessor, such a change takes about 0.5 second.

Similar statements can be made of other graphical manipulations: zooming, shrinking, and duplicating. There is a trend toward introducing new graphics *primitives*, the basic commands, embedded in the system, on which system functioning depends.

There is an accelerating change in applications development technology. Beyond evolutionary advances, the sort of product we can envision is a graphic tool that resembles computer-aided design and manufacturing (CAD/CAM) and is oriented to higher-order software. This is the whole sense of visual thinking.

Much more important, artificial intelligence will change not only the software industry but also the whole computer and communications domain. In the beginning, the products to be offered will tie into the current software industry structure by front-ending other companies' software. Still, the most fundamental change will come from knowledge-based *expert systems* (Esystems). They will lead to a qualitative change in how people use computers, and a knowledge-processing business that rivals the conventional data processing business in size will develop.

Menus, Windows, and Icons

Let's look in an orderly way at display functions, beginning with basic characteristics. One of the important issues associated with video display is the ability to dissociate:

- The scratch pad function from menu selection
- Menu selection from reporting

Another technical aspect is the simultaneous presentation of tabular data and the corresponding graphs. Color, smooth scrolling, and absence of jittering are musts.

The use of text associated with data and graphics displays can be divided into two major classes:

- Title: infopage, column, section, and so on
- Trim: comments and possible instructions

Menus create a routing path with mechanics that are transparent to the user. But it is also a recommended practice to build into the system a way to bypass the menu sequence and call up the required infopage in a *direct* way. A typical full-page menu will offer up to ten options, but it is good policy to use fewer than that and leave room for expansion. Since options (the routing pages) and the final infopage are presented in page form, it is wise to organize the information in the database in a page format, each page probably being identified. Page numbering must be done in a way which:

- Is easy to access
- Offers more than one database entry possibility

- Is open to expansion
- Can handle a variety of applications without changing page form

Also advisable is a two-way organization of the menu sequence contained in the database. The infopage will be found at the end of the tree and may contain tabular data, text, graphics, or other form of presentation. Normal menus can be designed by the user, but a pop-up menu will be built into the system. It will offer system commands as options to be visually selected and will usually offer three to five alternatives. This leads to the concepts of

- *Visual thinking*
- *Visual programming*

With visual programming, "What you see is what you get." The user defines a screen and associates it with an expression without having to worry about file handling and structure. This is done through a high-level interface. The processing of data will be done by generators.

User interfaces don't have to be sacred. Like any other technology, they need study, design, testing, and changing. The Xerox Star, for example, has undergone 30 different tests which led to significant findings. The lessons which were learned led to the development of principles for better design of the enabling technologies at the:

1. PC level, relative to the use of the local processor
2. LAN, for servers and interconnect
3. Bit-mapped display
4. The design and use of the mouse

The principles in user interface design are outlined in Table 20.

Visual programming has prerequisites. Research in user interface prototypes must be done; functional specifications must be developed, interface analysis must be done; and the user-oriented design and testing must be properly documented. Throughout the research, user actions must be predicted. The amount of user time and fatigue must be calculated. An experimental design should reflect real life situations. Figure 24 gives an example.

In the Xerox research, the functional tests included selection schemes, keyboard layout, display organization, icons, graphics, labels, property sheets, tabulation, help, prompt, and menu. The mouse was studied in regard to the number of keys which would assure the most user-friendly environment for making selections. Having assigned a specific function per key—get word, take sentence, fetch paragraph (Figure

TABLE 20   Visual thinking

Principles	Features
Explicit user's model	Desktop presentation
	Icons
	Windows
Seeing and pointing	Mouse
	Menus
	Pop-up menus
Universal commands*	Insert
	Delete
	Copy
	Move
	Show properties

* Other universal commands are help, search, change, exit, escape, end.

NOTE: The principle is, what we see is what we get.

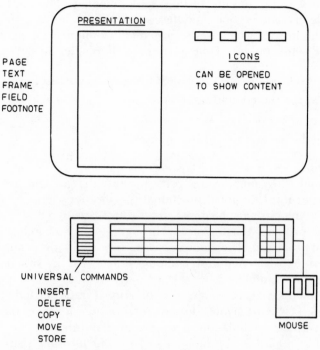

FIGURE 24.   An experimental design of visual programming.

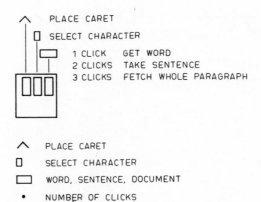

PLACE CARET
SELECT CHARACTER
1 CLICK   GET WORD
2 CLICKS TAKE SENTENCE
3 CLICKS FETCH WHOLE PARAGRAPH

PLACE CARET
SELECT CHARACTER
WORD, SENTENCE, DOCUMENT
• NUMBER OF CLICKS
→ DRAWTHROUGH - ADJUST

TESTS CONSIDERED:
- SELECTION TIME
- ERRORS BY FUNCTIONAL CLASS

BEST RESULTS:
- FIRST SELECT
- THEN DRAW

FIGURE 25. Mouse key selection schemes.

25)—the researchers examined user response. Tests included selection time and errors by functional class. The two-button scheme assigning

- First key to select
- Second key to draw

got the best results. With this scheme response times were shorter and there were fewer errors.

At the same time, Apple has suggested that the main reason for sticking to one key is to retain the option to use another device such as a graphic tablet. Another reason is that control keys on the mouse also have hysteresis (delay time), and there can be software problems in the use of multiple keys.

Visual Programming

Like the Xerox research, Apple's approach to visual programming rests on experimentation. The principle is the same. User interface design

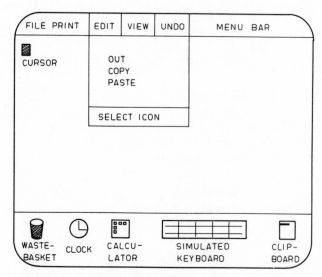

FIGURE 26. Visual programming approaches sustained by bit-mapping on a high-resolution video.

is determined by experimentation, not by following dogmatic principles. It is also a process that develops with steady practice and the observance of do's and don'ts. The current state-of-the-art approaches to visual programming, sustained through bit-mapping on a high-resolution video, can be outlined as in Figure 26.

At the top are the system commands being supported, including an example of a pop-up menu. At the bottom are the icons: wastebasket (to reset active memory), clock, calculator, simulated keyboard, and clipboard (to store for further retrieval). As applications experience accumulates, these elementary tools will no doubt have significant development. But we will never reach that level of development without steady practice. We must apply the tools we have available to reach the next level of sophistication.

At the time of writing, a major technological issue was the *logical support for windows*. More precisely, window management makes feasible a distribution between *physical* and *logical windows*. A physical window displays one or more pages of a document which can be manipulated in a logical sense. Logical support should definitely include a multiwindow manager able to:

1. *Scroll* up, down, left, right

2. *Command windows:* insert, delete, shrink, expand

3. *Turn pages:* next, preceding, by one, two, three, or more steps

The latter command makes it feasible to *browse* through documents under user command. It helps in running menus, and it handles imbedded applications.

Windows can be presented on the screen in overlays or by tiling, according to the software which is available. As the word suggests, tiling divides the screen into distinct windows, each of them specific to a job or mission. With screens of the size and resolution current in 1985, this is too restrictive in an applications sense. A better solution is overlays, which present the user with multiple overlapping windows. The active window on which the user works

- Has scroll bars
- Owns the menu bar and keyboard
- Is always on top

Figure 27 gives an example of multiple overlapping windows. The top line has system commands; the bottom line icons. The rest of the screen is dedicated to text and data presentation through windows selected by the user and displayed by the system.

The next most important challenge in end user software is document creation and filing. Workstation software should support the ability to:

- Create a document
- Create a folder

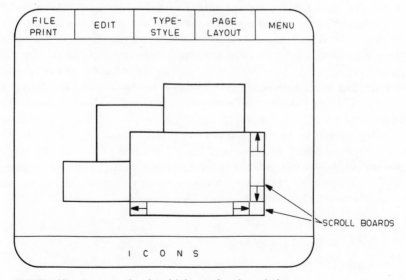

FIGURE 27. An example of multiple overlapping windows.

- Duplicate the document
- Insert the document in a folder to file it
- Drop the stationery into a wastebasket (tear it off)
- Monitor the printer if a hardcopy is desired

The importance of document-handling software must not be over-looked. Office automation will not get anywhere unless efficient solutions to document-handling problems are found.

There are two approaches to document-handling integration:

1. Have one applications package do everything
2. Move text, data, and graphics from one application to another in a transparent manner

Both approaches lead to the same result: being able to get results by merging text, data, and graphics. Data transfer and consistency of commands are issues addressed by the integrated software.

In practical terms, one solution is to provide an abstract machine in which the visual interface acts as a toolbox. This supports visual consistency but does not assure consistency of commands. When more memory is available, it is possible to precode standard commands. The applications programming (AP) must only provide the linkage routines. In any case, software modules must be built with the view to integrating them in a given environment.

The need for standards is self-evident. Both the designers of the vendor firm and the system specialists of the user organization should have a high degree of consistency. It is necessary to assure standard commands for data, text, and pictures. These standards can be universal. When nonstandard commands are employed, not only must the programmers agree on how to communicate information between their modules but translator routines must also be employed. This tends to introduce delays, errors, and inconsistencies and leads to confusion at the user side.

The fact that at the user level of the International Standards Organization Open System Interconnection model (ISO/OSI) no standards have yet been worked out leaves each vendor with the freedom to choose a different frame of reference. Most vendors do, however, agree that menu commands in simple English are needed:

- File and/or print
- Edit/typestyle paper layout
- Undo last change
- Duplicate

- Copy
- File
- Clear

If the menu is a pop-up, the system command can be selected simply by positioning the cursor on the chosen line by means of the mouse. Mouse-and-menu coordination requires a well-established syntax to enable the user to make selection consistent.

Menus as Natural Languages

The term "natural language" is used to identify a human language as contrasted to a computer language. Menus are not actually in natural language; but because they use plain English and/or icons, they exhibit midway characteristics. One of the important features of the menu approach is that the user needs no training to communicate with the computer. In that sense, menus present a *natural link* supported by associated software.

Therefore, the use of menu solutions aims to reduce the skill and training requirements of man-machine communication. These are the basics:

- Easy user education.
- Structured applications development
- Screen management conditioned by the menu
- Natural link interface

Training for sufficient expertise to work comfortably in a computer environment can demand 1 to 2 years for PL/1 or Cobol, a month or two for formal query command structure, and a couple of days with interactive screen capability through a mouse and menus—using the mouse as a pointer device.

In its current status, a natural link interface presents the user with a series of menus displayed on video. Each menu offers a variety of options. The user can manipulate windows designated as *active*. A choice is made by placing the cursor over the desired item in a pop-up menu. The feature that most distinguishes a solid approach to natural link technology is the assurance that a user can compose only a valid command for the computer (Figure 28). That is because, in the directing process, the user is presented with all the valid choices, and only with valid choices, one of which is selected.

To support the user in an able manner, the natural link requires

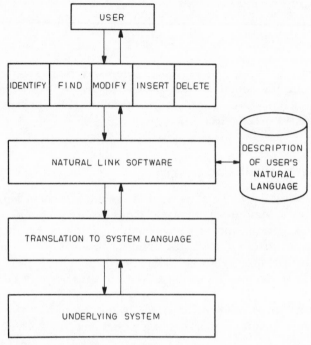

FIGURE 28. Natural language interaction.

specific ways of input. First is a grammar that defines how the options can be combined and how they can be mapped into the target language of the computer. Second is a lexicon defining the text associated with the target language as well as the text to be displayed on the screen. Third is a screen description specifying the placement and content of all menus.

A relational database with a data dictionary can help to automatically derive much of the specific information required to complete the interface. Among the advantages at the end user level we find:

1. The ability to recognize the desired option readily
2. The ease in constructing acceptable commands
3. The elimination of unanswerable questions and/or alternatives
4. The fact that the underlying code is more efficient
5. The equally important fact that spelling and typing problems are eliminated and error checking is minimized

Better results can be obtained by enforcing compatibility of grammar, lexicon, and screen description. Specification of the grammar determines the components of the user input language. Each terminal component must have a corresponding entry in the lexicon to permit mapping into the target language of the computer system.

- Lexicon contents are a function of the grammar.
- If the grammar or the lexicon is changed, a corresponding change must be made in the other.
- If correspondence of grammar and lexicon is not maintained, the interface will behave unpredictably.

Another must is to assure the correctness of the screen description. Within the screen description, window descriptors define the characteristics of an individual window. They typically include the display coordinates, size, and contents of the window.

To facilitate quick and easy changes in a window, the system keeps the descriptors in a file rather than embedded in software. New descriptors can be added to the file, existing ones can be modified, and old ones can easily be deleted when no longer needed. A screen is a set of windows. Operations that affect membership in the screen are screen-level. Operations that affect only the characteristics of a single window are window-level.

Basic options to be supported are add, edit, copy, delete:

Add window adds a new window descriptor to the screen description.

Edit permits the user to modify an existing window descriptor.

Copy enables the user to create a new window descriptor based on the characteristics of an existing one.

Delete enables the user to delete a window descriptor from the screen descriptor.

To make the screen function, we use a set of window descriptors to create a display on the video device. *Load screen* elicits the path name under which a descriptor has been stored and loads the descriptor into the memory. Loading the screen descriptor into memory, controlling screen input/output, invoking the processing of user input, invoking the translator to map the user input into target language, passing target language to the underlying computer system, and handling data from the computer system to the output screen are operations related to the execution of the interface. This process requires a collection of callable procedures which provide a unified, easily understood means of controlling execution.

The interface should provide other ease-of-use features, such as *help facilities*. The user may at any time ask for help concerning the item on which the cursor is currently placed. When that is done, a window should appear with the appropriate help message. Some of the help text could be automatically generated at interface generation time; but to be most effective, some help text will have to be provided by the analysts and the database administrator.

Another menu feature is automatic search as an alternative to scrolling for selection from windows containing a lengthy list of items. The user should do nothing more than type a printable key. Still another feature is *back tracking,* which permits the user to back out of a query or a process by using a restart or quit function.

For *error prevention* purposes, the user should be guided through query composition. As one element of a query is selected, additional potential selections must be narrowed down to remain consistent with the current state of the query. The user should be kept informed as to whether or not the query can be executed.

To summarize, a screen or window should permit the user to specify what it should look like. A message builder should allow the user to call for help, receive prompts or have error messages, and attach a help message to a particular item or window within a screen description. The user should also get assistance in testing the interface.

As an example, we will follow menus and prompts with a word processing software. Most of the important activities are accomplished through menu selection; others are accessed by response to prompts, by instructions given to the operator, or by function keys.

Attention must be given to learning about major menus and about some of the most frequently used prompts in the system. Detailed instruction about each separate selection in these menus must be given as the user progresses through the training exercises. The main menu permits access to all the major functions available. Certain of these selections lead to secondary menus; others bring a series of prompts to the screen. Responding to a prompt or instruction completes the action. The main menu includes:

EDIT an existing document

CREATE a new document

SPELL: check spelling in a document

PRINT or review a document

DELETE documents

GLOSS: glossary functions

AUX: auxiliary functions

LANG: select language change

EXIT from the subsystem

EDIT brings the *edit document name* prompt to the screen. It is needed for editing a document. CREATE displays the *format options menu* for the selection of a format (for creating a new document). SPELL displays the *spelling options* menu to check the spelling of words in a document. PRINT displays the *print review functions* menu.

DELETE permits deletion of a document from the directory. GLOSS displays the *glossary functions* menu for work with abbreviation glossaries. AUX displays the *auxiliary functions* menu. LANG selects language change. EXIT takes the system out of the WP package and returns it to the operating system level.

COPY IN and COPY OUT functions allow the user to create sentences, paragraphs, or pages of often-used material and store them for recall when needed. The same COPY feature can be used to copy a portion of material, a column, or even a single sentence to another area within a document or to another document.

Experimenting on User-Oriented Design

Tools are needed to model the user's task. The job of the interface is to contribute a software and hardware (SW/HW) support and, through it, man-machine interactivity. Even in a small project, user interfaces are important. They involve:

1. Screen abstraction
2. Command tuning
3. Database accesses
4. Icon library
5. Software routines
6. User function library

Modeling involves *formal linguistics* including a finite-state machine, transition planning, parser, and *artificial intelligence* (AI)—most particularly knowledge-based systems.

AI-oriented production language programming induces us to move control structures out of the classical flowcharts of computer programs and into declarative forms. This leads to free evolution processes and incremental development. As discussed in the appropriate chapter, knowledge-based systems will make it possible to write better software through computer assistance.

We have reached the limits of man-based software development. Throwing ten times as many programmers at a project will not guarantee a program ten times as good; it will virtually guarantee something that is worse. It could be in the computer's power to overcome product development failings.

A critical component of the AI-based software solution is comprehensive hand-holding and support to users. The product must work as an aggregate. And it must work well. Continuity is another vital issue that expert systems can be expected to solve. Current software is characterized by completely disposable policies. New product releases often do not relate to their predecessors at all. Expert systems can be expected to integrate operating system and applications software and thereby provide an evolutionary path.

The dual goal is to *increase the productivity of the programming process and the quality of the program product.* The key components in automating the development process are:

1. A very high level language (fourth or fifth generation)
2. An advanced database management system
3. An intelligent editor and reusable software library

The process involves

- Nonprocedural statements in 4GL or 5GL
- Translation of 4GL descriptions into a set of specifications for program components
- Retrieval of appropriate components from the reusable library
- Generation of new components as necessary
- Elimination of file management, because this is handled by the database management systems (DBMS)
- Integration of the software components into an executable program

Thus the basic attributes are the very high level language (fifth generation), the reusable software components, and the methodology to go about them. This mode of operation permits rapid prototyping based on automatic program generation. The range of tools can be impressive.

- *Spreadsheets* for managerial applications
- *SQL, Ingres, Mapper* for business applications
- *APL* and *CAD/CAM* for engineering and scientific applications
- *Prolog* for compiler writing
- *Unix/C-Shell* for system building

Although the tools are available, their usage has so far been the exception rather than the rule. Most companies still stick to the obsolete

TABLE 21   A comprehensive policy beyond the adoption of 4GL

1. *Develop user-oriented software design.* Not only coinvolve the end user but build the system *for the user.*

2. *Invest in people.* Analysts and programmers, like programs, *need maintenance.* Train to keep up morale and productivity.

3. *Encourage innovation.* We live in a time of rapid evolution. Don't stick to old images.

4. *Use small, expert teams.* Many great software products are produced by small groups of people. (Examples are Unix, APL, and Pascal.)

5. *Invest in automated software engineering practices.* This should start with management practices, include methodology, and be applied throughout the organization. [The typical American system analyst/programmer (SA/P) is supported by $25,000 in capital investment; the typical Japanese SA/P by $35,000.]

6. *Commit to quality.* Institute a quality board; use independent quality assurance teams. Perform regular postmortems. Forbid programmers to perform changes during a unit test. (About 20 percent of code is changed during a unit test.)

7. *Establish firm software engineering practices.* This should start with management practices, include methodology, apply throughout the organization, and *institute technology transfer.* It should include:
   - Design reviews
   - Postmortems
   - Uniformity
   - Feedbacks

215

high-level languages (Cobol, Fortran, and so on), and the results are low programmer productivity, high production costs, slippages in time schedules, and very high maintenance costs.

But the adoption of a 4GL, although necessary, is not enough to change the software development images prevailing in an organization. The comprehensive policy outlined in Table 21 is necessary. Notice that the number 1 item beyond the adoption of sophisticated, very high level tools is emphasis on the end user. Not only should the user be an integral part of the design picture but also, as we should never forget, the databasing, data communications, data processing, and word processing system is made *for* the user.

Interactive design of user interfaces makes the task a communications art. The design should profit from study of good communications from writers, film makers, artists, and even video game designers. The designer should not make the work as dry and boring as reading a telephone book. Moreover, he or she will also have to look quite actively for fair compromises: For every "principle" of interface design, there exists an opposite "principle"—and there are no universal, well-established rules.

The basic methodology should be an interaction of synthetic, analytic, and testing modules. We have to look at the problem, imagine solution(s), identify the far-out problems created by the solutions, develop alternatives, try to optimize, and test for results. The goal is to get insight. Not numbers.

CHAPTER 15

The Drive toward Graphics Applications

An order that can be misunderstood, will be misunderstood.

ARMY AXIOM

Information in graphics format is comprehended quickly. With graphics we are able to run our businesses smarter and more accurately by identifying trends and deviations. Changes in a course of action and snags in plans can be detected immediately.

In contrast, presenting the same data in pages and volumes of tabular formats is a turnoff. The precision of the single number may be enhanced, but the accuracy of the aggregate suffers. Presented with tabular forms, the executive always tries to convert numbers to orders of magnitude, trends, and exceptions. Why not offer that information—in charts—in the first place?

If the information system's mission is to provide management with better information faster, a key question should be: How can management get this information in a meaningful action-oriented way? The best way to add value to management information is to present the information in a format that makes it simple to understand and interpret. That means getting into graphics.

Another benefit derived from the graphics approach is that managers and professionals are becoming more familiar with computers. This helps improve profitability and performance. By giving the end user direct access to the information tools that will minimize errors, we make the organization more responsive to its environment.

It is true that charting can also be done manually by the planning and analysis department, which compiles the data and prepares the management reports, but manual approaches are slow and inefficient. Computer-based solutions can turn out a large number of up-to-the-minute charts very rapidly, and the computer has the ability to analyze trends and present different views of the data. Furthermore, in a graphic form inaccurate data will show up. The database can be pruned and the whole reporting process tuned to the end user's needs.

The user can participate by looking for alternatives in evaluation and presentation, using color to differentiate, underline, and flash out exceptions, and obtaining needed information interactively without programming knowledge or computer specialist background. And the best part of the computer-aided presentation is that it can be updated so easily.

Three Levels of Computer Graphics

Computer graphics is destined to be a major part of office automation systems. The key trends in the business computer graphics field include a user's perspective as well as an executive overview. At the same time, because of high-resolution graphics and visual thinking concepts, a three-way division is developing:

1. Charts
2. Complex graphics
3. Icons

Charts are of the bar, line, and pie type. They represent the more classical approach to management graphics which, in a PC environment, is spreadsheet-oriented. Charting solutions can be nicely presented with low-resolution video screens such as those featured with the first and early second generations of personal computers (PCs). Videotex is another graphics presentation means, and alphamosaics pose no problems.

The value of charting is in its presentation and the attention it gets and in its ability to point to corrective action. Charting can have different levels of sophistication in presentation. Smart people who use color charts *standardize* the color. Multiple charts per page can be a help in the presentation: We need more flexibility in the graphics system than in the classical reporting system. More complex computer graphics call for six basic components of support:

1. Greater computer power
2. Appropriate software
3. Proper resolution in output equipment
4. Needed input data
5. Capable user interfaces
6. A training program able to change user images

The most exciting field is the sixth, because it must alter established concepts. Even in the most evolved organizations, presentation today is 60 percent on paper, 20 percent on video, and 20 percent on other means such as transparencies and slides. Furthermore, video is particularly used for self-presentation and paper and transparencies for presentation to others.

This also bears on the fact that multicommunications capabilities are now only taking off. An estimated 50 percent of applications in 1984 were on stand-alone micros. Another 25 percent of PCs were used as nonintelligent terminals. Downloading with local processing is a relevant activity for the other 25 percent. The trend is to increase this kind of use.

Although the quality of artistic work with the first- and second-generation micros is not great, the graphics capability of the 32-bit PC is first class. At the same time, an increasing number of firms no longer want to use a large mainframe as a controller for graphics. If equal to or greater than 0.6-Mpixel (mega, or million, pixel), resolution, an alpha-geometric-alphaphotographic presentation is the rule for good-quality graphics. For hardcopy output, laser is the solution. Such units take 20 seconds for a job the classical plotter needs 30 minutes to do.

Examples of complex graphics are engineering designs of all kinds—drafting, architectural plans, machine diagrams, artistic views—and also type quality, italics, boldface, and so on—for document handling.

Icons could be equated to complex graphics, but I put them in a separate class for two reasons.

- The first is because *icon shapes* can be used as standard modules in visual thinking
- The second is because capable handling of icon interfaces calls for a query language

Icon shapes may be associated with naming tests. The latter are needed when, with visual thinking, we must select from a set of icons, make yes or no identification, or pick one from a group.

In current practice, the presentation of icons can vary widely. The challenge is how the population of users associates semantics with them. The best presentation is the *simple icon;* the worst presentations are sophisticated designs (because of too many errors) and those including literary descriptions (because of slow reaction by the user).

Graphics tests are necessary to measure the effectiveness of icons. The usual measures are time needed to do a drawing, type of available line commands, critical incidents, problems being presented, and training ease. Online examples and associated tests are the only way to debug the system. Lessons learned in this type of implementation suggest it is wise to:

1. Develop selection schemes
2. Do a detailed comparison
3. Test the icons
4. Use videotape for feedback to designers
5. Establish verbal protocols (ask people what they think)
6. Not be afraid to redesign

At the same time, proper attention must be given to icon interfaces. In an integrated approach, icon selection and menu processing will be associated with a *canonical query language* (CQL). The functioning to be supported rests on the translation of icons into CQL subsets (functionally specialized). If this implementation is universal over a network of workstations, mainframes, and databases, a wealth of information elements can be accessed by the user. A basic rule is to utilize as much commodity software as possible and require very little change—or, better, none at all. Another basic rule is to make the whole process PC-based.

Among the presentation services which should be available at the WS are screen management, menu handling, icon interpretation, editing facilities, and compilation. The role of the host system should be that of serving as *control center*. Control center functions can be related to complex graphics and icons in several ways. As more text, data, and image presentations proliferate at the workstation (WS) level, we need a resource to manage the consistency. It is also very important to assure the integrity of the corporate data is not violated.

Redundant data must be provided in an information resource management operation. This must be done as a prerequisite—covering both the integrity of information resources and the system commands, icons, and graphics definitions.

Using Management Graphics

As the uses of PC-based graphics have proliferated, many organizations have evaluated the results they obtain. Such studies have established that the results are indeed positive and that they range from productivity gains to marketing supports:

1. Visuals affect business meetings.

In an analytical study with a control group and the same arguments, 67 percent voted for a proposal when it was given visual presentation but only 50 percent when it was not. Also, graphs can highlight trends and patterns before detailed discussion begins. If changes are needed in a chart during a meeting, it is possible to turn out a presentation-quality graph in a few seconds with PC-supported approaches.

2. Graphics help make decisions immediate.

A research project has confirmed that graphics help make a point. They lead to hard dollar savings because they focus on the subject, outline trends, reduce uncertainty, and increase comprehension. Information in graphic format is comprehended quickly. Significant trends can be spotted immediately. When the same data is presented in tabular form, important trends are difficult to spot.

3. Graphics assist in exception reporting.

A *visual early warning system* through realtime charting sharpens the executive's ability to comprehend complex situations. Computer graphics can quickly summarize massive quantities of data into meaningful information. In the past, executives, engineers, or analysts would have to pore over tables of numbers for hours. Now the information from those tables can be viewed immediately, and exceptions can be flashed out.

One company wanted graphics capability to simplify the task of analyzing balance-sheet items of assets and liabilities. In its regular review meetings, management goes through a detailed analysis of trends in the balance sheets. It looks at some forty graphs per meeting. When management is talking of trends, making projections, or exercising control, the magnitude of differences is much more evident in graphs. "Without the ability to produce graphs easily and quickly, we could never get as much done in our meetings," an executive has commented.

4. Graphics can help in marketing proposals and client presentation.

When they use graphics, sales engineers are perceived as more credible and interesting and also as more professional and better prepared—hence persuasive. One company provided its sales representatives with PC and graphics packages. The salespeople had no prior computer experience, yet they learned to develop schematic diagrams in a few hours. The company then added some training in conventions for accessing the displays. Now the people who create the displays are those who will be using them. And that is a very effective approach.

5. Computer graphics affect the cost of presentation.

A given presentation study done in the classical way cost $90 per page; a comparable one done with computer graphics cost $2 per page. Similarly, the cost of a single slide drops from $35 to $7.50. General Motors had an interesting experience along this line. In 1977 charting for the board required sixteen people: nine for designing and seven for proofing. Today the job is fully automated. Another large organization wasted 54 labor-years per year to do reporting and charting which has now been fully automated.

But graphics can also be a two-edged knife. As an expert in the field has said, there are three areas in which you should not fool around: brain surgery, parachuting, and computer graphics.

What is the difference between success and failure in graphics? The answer can be given in two words: preparation and quality. As for preparation, it is unwise to start from the beginning and produce a new chart each time. The rational way is to use the database: call up the existing chart and make improvements and changes. As for quality, by 1976 we had *publications quality* graphics with computer-based systems, though the existing supports were low-grade by today's standards. Presently, graphics is the one area in which quality comes to the attention of everybody.

Quality is a presentation issue, and it is in full evolution. What is sophisticated today will be standard tomorrow. To improve both preparation and presentation quality, an *action plan* is necessary. The first step is to improve access. The key to graphics is to make the facility accessible to everybody in the organization. The second step is to offer chartbooks; it is unwise to start from scratch. The third is to provide data links, and the fourth is to assure briefings. Users react to them better than to formal training. The difference is timing and duration. Briefings typically last 2 hours per week—not 5 days once a year.

The fifth step is to give technical assistance to the user population. The sixth is to keep the software current and steadily improve quality. Things don't happen because of an order. They happen when the users recognize their value and go for them.

Standards for Computer Graphics

We have come a long way from the early years of computer graphics, which were characterized by the development of devices rather than end user concepts. Though devices assisted in the introduction of computer graphics to many application areas, it is the implementation of computer graphics for the end user which has altered our approach.

Furthermore, in the 1970s practically all of the graphics systems were restricted to certain mainframe computers, to a given host language, and to specific graphics disciplines, computer-aided design and manufacturing (CAD/CAM) being the best known. Also, most of the systems addressed a single area of application.

Yet with the increasing use of computer graphics and with greater efficiency and reduced costs through the use of personal computers, the practice spread to management. Now the need is for a basis for the evaluation of systems for communication through graphics methods and for computer graphics education.

Computer graphics is typically associated with the computer *synthesis* of pictures: generating charts and icons with the aid of a digital computer. In contrast, the *analysis* of pictures is called *computer image processing*. Though the two activities have many features in common, they are different disciplines and should be treated as such.

Originally, computer graphics were useful in architecture, engineering, industrial design, visual perception, pattern recognition, computer image processing, map making and surveying, graphic design in the publishing industry, animated films whether for education or entertainment, and in a whole range of visual aids for education, presentation, and art. Business graphics is a relatively new vista offering broad perspectives in display technology.

Computer graphics education must present the history of those efforts and the milestones which have been passed. It is also advisable to explain that, with current technology, graphics are of two kinds:

1. **Interactive.** Program and data are entered in continuing man-machine dialog with changing picture output on the video display.

2. **Batch.** Program and data are input all at once, and the picture output is on film or paper.

The components of an interactive graphics system are diagrammed in Figure 29. They invariably include a data processor, computer interfaces, display hardware, interactive controls, graphics computer languages, the ability to present two- and three-dimensional data structures, generation of lines, curves, surfaces, and textures, and computer-based geometry.

A characteristic of graphics systems is that input and output can no longer be governed only by requirements of the program. Since they are the two components of a man-machine dialog, input and output must be adapted to the human operator. This means allowing for human

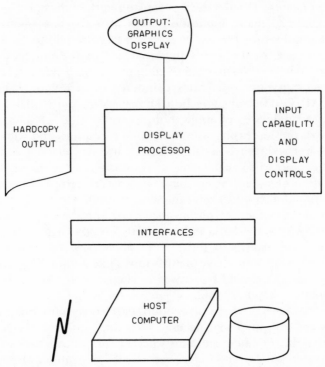

FIGURE 29. The components of an interactive graphics system.

errors without disastrous results, like abort, and not asking for data already known to the system. Hence, methods are necessary for supporting the design of good user interfaces. By means of dialog routines, the user must be reassured about the data already entered and informed on how it is processed by the system.

In other terms, computer graphics offer improved man-machine communication. This means a better, clearer, and faster perception of:

- Overall structure
- Fine detail
- Evident errors

At the same time, computer graphics permit interactive use. They not only replace tedious manual drawings but yield pictures that, with computer database help, can later be edited, revised, and given proper analysis and detailing. Related pictures can be generated from an original schema.

To improve the quality of a dialog, it is necessary to get monitoring data that always distinguishes between two different behaviors: that of the system and that of the user. By monitoring system behavior, we can obtain data about response time, error traces, frequency of command usage, structure of command sequences, and so on. Such information is obtained through state-of-the-art monitors. The study of user behavior has in the background the recognition that the operator is an integral part of the system and is also a very complex element critical to overall performance of the graphics system.

Let's look at this issue from the viewpoint of a fully automated aggregate. From point of origin to point of destination, the places where data originates must be identifiable in a unique way. Data must be provided to the monitor without changing the normal man-information communications procedures. Data values, such as the user-provided input, must be maintained and the text analyzed for comments and command sequences. It must also be possible to evaluate feedback as additional help in dialog procedures.

The dialog must be carried out within a uniform framework: Embedding of the dialog elements in a programming or specification language for the end user; providing an interpreter or compiler, which maps the language constructs to the functions at run time, and setting the format of the interface between the application program and the dialog system.

When that is achieved, the dialog aggregate can be used in a given application by adapting its input and output functions to the interface. For the dialog elements a syntax has to be defined, as well as a methodology for building a hierarchy of dialog parameters such as procedural concepts. There must also be a common control structure for dataflow. The graphics language should be easy to learn and its rules simple and consistent. It is desirable for the graphics system to have machine and device independence, and hence portability.

Standards for interactive computer graphics that are emerging might make both engineering and management graphics applications as widespread as spreadsheet and word processing. By promoting program portability, which makes it possible to run the same programs on different machines, standards will substantially enlarge the market for graphics products.

Eventually, the development of sophisticated graphics applications for personal workstations will be economically feasible. The benefit for the end user will be wider software offerings, higher quality at reduced cost, and the assistance interactive graphics can offer in his or her work.

Among the needed standards are:

- Programmer interfaces
- Device interfaces
- Generalized file interchange

A programmer interface has to do with the conceptual model and the syntax the programmer uses when incorporating graphics functions into an application program. It standardizes the calling sequence and functions of a graphics procedure library.

A device interface has to do with the protocol used for communication between the device-independent and the device-dependent functions. It defines a device driver protocol consistent with all graphics tools.

Management graphics presentation (in the current state of the art) does not require the resolution and complexity needed for computer-aided engineering. It is therefore quite advisable to adopt an international standard like the Presentation Level Protocol (NA/PLPS, CEPT/VPLPS) which is applicable for text, data, graphics, and images. Its use will permit standard exchanges and avoid the acrobatics of conversions of code sets, communications protocols, line disciplines, file structures, and presentation modes.

Generalized file transfer is still a different matter; it is necessary because of the plurality of devices we use. These devices are largely incompatible among themselves in respect to design features, including file structure.

Some people look at the Graphics Kernel System (GKS) as the principal emerging standard at the programmer level, but I believe it would be more correct to place it at the generalized file interchange level. Now let's look at the standardization effort for file interchange.

The Leading Standardization Effort

Since about 1970, the need for a generalized file transfer standard has been getting advocates. It got formal recognition at a meeting of the Special Interest Group on Computer Graphics of the Association for Computing Machinery (SIGGRAPH) held by the National Bureau of Standards (NBS) in 1974.

Three years later, in 1977, the Graphics Standards Planning Committee released its first draft: the SIGGRAPH Core Standard. It incorporated I/O capabilities for a range of graphics devices without, however, addressing the field of raster graphics, which is particularly prominent. The status report of this committee was released in 1979 at the annual SIGGRAPH conference. The Core Graphics System (CGS),* including methodology and specifications, was outlined. Most important, the concept of the *metafile* was outlined in the sense of *a device-independent picture*

---

* Also known as GSPC-Core, after the initials of the Graphics Standards Planning Committee.

file. Since then, the metafile has become a model for distributed graphics systems. It is a file about files. And *metadata* is data about data.

Let's be quite clear about the terminology:

- A standard able to support the basic graphics capabilities is the *core system.*
- The application dependent on the functioning of a core system is the *modeling system.*

Definition, transformations, calculations, storage, and retrieval of an engineering design or of complex management graphs are accomplished by the presentation of a model or models. The interactions with the user and the portability of the graphics files among devices is the task of the core system.

A core system should be independent of the computer, the specific graphics devices, the programming language(s) being employed, and also the applications area. It should be based on a generally agreed-upon reference model (Figure 30). It should also provide a uniform basis for education in computer graphics, and the graphics metafiles should provide a standard interface for storage and transfer of graphical

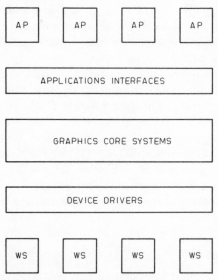

FIGURE 30. A core system should be independent of the computer, the specific graphics devices, the programming language(s) being employed, and also the applications area. It should be based on a generally agreed-upon reference model.

information. It was largely on the basis of those concepts that the standardization work went ahead.

Following the 1979 SIGGRAPH Annual Conference, the American National Standards Institute (ANSI) created Technical Committee X3H3 for Computer Graphics Programming Languages. This is now the foremost graphics standardization body in America. At the same time (1976 to 1979), in Germany, Subcommittee NI-5.9 of the Deutsches Institut für Normung (DIN) was working on a similar standardization effort which led to the Graphics Kernel System (GKS). Today the GKS is the principal emerging standard for graphics file interchange.

Whereas the CGS was intended to be a comprehensive three-dimensional standard, GKS is two-dimensional and is aimed at the basic graphics functions. That is a fundamental reason why the International Standards Organization (ISO) working group on computer graphics* selected it in 1979 as the basis for a worldwide standard—after evaluating both CGS and GKS.

The GKS has felt the influence of many national standards organizations: ANSI, AFNOR (France), BSI (England), NNI (Holland). Now a Draft International Standard (DIS) has been promoted for the reason that it allows portability of graphics applications between different computers by providing a consistent interface. Typically this interface reflects a high-level language: Fortran, Pascal, et al. The standard also improves a programmer's ability to work on different systems: it supports a full set of drawing primitive commands with variable attributes, as well as device-independent picture segments.

Because of a comprehensive set of area-filling and pixel-array primitives, GKS is ideal for raster graphics. A major plus is the standard interfacing between the application programs and the graphics utility programs, while the Virtual Device Interface (VDI) standardizes the interchange between graphics utilities and device drivers (Figure 31).

The GKS provides device independence for standard functions. Nonstandard operations are made available through the Generalized Drawing Primitive. This is a defined mechanism for escape from GKS; it permits access to the particular capabilities of a nonstandard device.

Technical Notes

Alphamosaic, *alphageometric,* and *alphaphotographic* have to do with the definition with which images are reflected on computer screens. The crudest representations are produced by using the combinations at which

---

* TC97/SC5/WG2

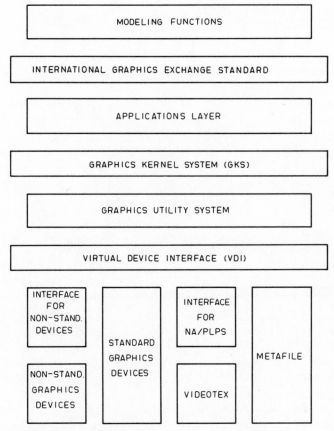

FIGURE 31. The Virtual Device Interface standardizes the exchange between graphics utilities and device drivers.

we arrive through the division of a character into a mosaic form. Better images are produced by point-to-point construction, which can approximate picture quality.

Icons are representations of familiar objects. They are the oldest language of mankind. In ancient Egypt and Babylonia they were used as written means of expressing languages, known as hieroglyphics. Such pictorial writing continues to be used, as by the Chinese, and now we find it in traffic signs in the west. Icons are one of the means of making personal computers "user-friendly" in the sense of communication between the user and the information which is stored and handled by the machine.

CHAPTER 16

The New Services

Knowledge has become performance, and this means rapid change.

PETER DRUCKER

Twenty-five years of computer experience made us appreciate that knowing how to operate large machines and networks or build elegant systems which provide the most efficient hardware and software is only part of the information problem. The real issue is how to solve business problems by making information work for the people who need it. Distributed processing, networking, the database challenge, and computers and communications in general can be put in those simple terms.

The starting point is understanding how information capabilities are delivered to and received by the end users. That requires a knowledge of the business—how it operates and what its important features are. The implementation process for computers, databases, and data communications involves several phases (Figure 32):

1. Gaining management's recognition and acceptance from the beginning

2. Obtaining a commitment to the tangible and intangible costs of change

3. Involving the end user in the design of the change

4. Improving productivity in a stepwise, documented manner

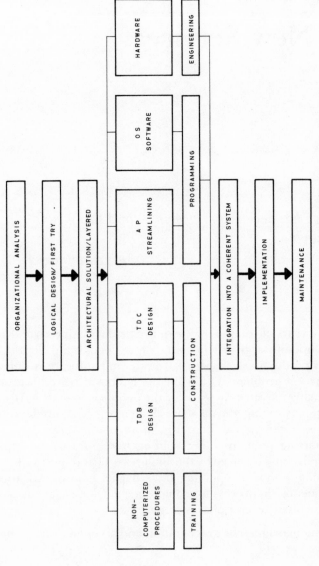

FIGURE 32. Phases in the implementation of computers, databases, and data communications.

5. Acquiring technologies that match needs and that people will accept

6. Designing man-machine interfaces and limiting the impact on organizational structures and relationships

7. Keeping costs lower than the benefits derived

8. Implementing the change effectively (with appropriate training and sales effort)

9. Planning the gradual evolution of information technology within the organization

10. Training the user to the new system and demonstrating cost and benefit in a simple, efficient, understandable manner

Among the factors that contribute to the success of a systems development project, the most important is the participation of the end user. The success of the system is directly related to the user's involvement. That is often overlooked by management because of the highly technical nature of computer systems and the attitude that "systems development should be the responsibility of a computer specialist."

Whether we want to accept it or not, many things have changed during the last few years in our profession. A distributed environment will allow maximal accessibility to data resources while providing for a high degree of sharing of costly equipment. And it is becoming increasingly apparent that data requirements, performance, and availability are inseparable from good business organization and are vital tools in the marketplace.

Current objectives and future goals are not necessarily the same thing. As far as we can see today, the objectives to be served through properly designed, distributed, and interactive databases range from a reduction in personnel costs, through higher productivity, to the control of communications costs and an increase in computer availability to the user.

Advances in computer, communications, and database technology steadily emphasize the desirability of dedicating applications to stand-alone mini- and microcomputers with or without the benefit of a private network. This provides end users with the ability to control their own resources and service levels while isolating the users from effects of unpredictable blackout in central computer capabilities or changes in timesharing priority beyond their control.

What the different efforts currently underway say between the lines is that in the decade of the 1980s the problem is not only the network but also, if not mainly, the terminal. And the main challenge will be not technology, but cost. When hundreds of terminals will be used at a certain site (local network) it will be necessary to coordinate them and interface them to the long-haul network. This brings into view the issue of the computer-based private branch exchange (PBX).

The Office of Tomorrow

The automated office of the coming years will not be devoid of people, but it will be practically free of paperwork—whether that paper is the result of data, voice, or any other type of communication inside or outside the organization. The physical productivity chores of the automated office will be done with or by advanced microprocessor-supported tools. In the international money transfer department of New York's Citibank, 50 people sitting before desktop computer terminals handle the work that 430 people performed in 1970.

New office products are coming along. As recent information indicates, executives may be talking to typewriters and getting written responses as early as 1986. The first commercial voice-activated typewriters, known as VATs, cost about $25,000, but the time savings can be significant and the price will drop sharply by the end of the decade. The initial VATs, benefitting from faster-than-expected technical advances, will come from IBM, Xerox, and Matsushita; they will correctly recognize about 95 percent of "typical" business English as spoken by the average executive. Each VAT will be equipped with a screen which displays the words as they are spoken.

This relatively paperfree office—a headquarters facility, branch house, manufacturing plant, field sales office, or any other operational unit—will have as a "central nervous system," the private branch exchange (PBX). The PBX will become the gate of the automated office to the communications network; it will provide the main switching gear for all types of compunications from data and text to image and voice.

Before too long, we will see families of computer-based PBXs acting as the new elements in the distributed information processing marketplace of the 1980s, primarily as managers of local networks. By offering customers a product that manages *both* its voice communications and its local data network (LAN), the PBX could significantly enhance technology leadership and market position and provide the user with the ability to lower telecommunications costs. Examples are:

- *Toll restrictions.* Certain user stations can be prevented from making toll calls.
- *Least-cost routing.* The lowest-cost toll route can be selected automatically.
- *Call detail recording.* A log of all toll calls is made by user.

- *Direct inward dialing.* Incoming calls bypass the operator.
- *Automatic call distribution.* Incoming calls to order clerks or reservations are evenly distributed among workers.
- *Electronic message services.* The user can attach keyboard screen terminals and printers to the PBX for the purpose of forwarding the text messages.

Typically, a PBX consists of a number of information transmission, switching, and storage services. What is most important, it is directly linked to and interactive with all other offices in the organization through a network of other PBXs and multifunctional computer-supported workstations. The distributed information system could not have a better example than that.

The branch exchange (public or private) had a relatively slow development in its early years (following Strowger's basic discovery). We have reached the present-day electronic PBX through successive modernizations which accelerated in the late 1960s. By 1978 to 1980, all major telephone manufacturers had developed computer-based PBX equipment, a solution that presented both significant advantages and some constraints. Among the advantages were reduced space, rapid installation, greater reliability, and autodiagnostics.

Computer-based PBXs make the integration of voice and data feasible, and in this chapter that opens two lines of thought:

1. In the old, telephony-oriented approach, data is subsidiary to voice and is collected through a dedicated processor.
2. In the modern, integrated approach, computer-based machines treat voice, data, and text equally.

With teletex and compunication systems, the reader may view only principal statements or all statements down to a preestablished level. Once written, the text may be joined to other texts in the system and then formatted. A dictionary will typically be available to correct spelling errors. The text may be protected (stored in an electronic notebook), distributed informally as a message, or used to generate camera-ready copy complete with graphics and color instructions. Users working together may view and edit separate texts on split screens.

Eventually, text changes will be made via simple English-like mnemonic commands (copy, create, insert) entered over a standard keyboard or with a cord-and-mouse set that allows the user to move a cursor around the screen and enter simple commands over a binary version of a court reporter's steno machine. In short, the merger of technologies into an office automation system will not only be at the level of the mechanics (this is self-evident with voice digitization) but will also, and mainly, be at the conceptual level of the future evolution of technology.

An Integrated Approach

Integrated, cost-cutting methods and equipment are sorely needed, and this is well documented by the cost of producing a single typed page in the United States—about $9.50 in 1978, about $12 in 1984, and still on the way up. Also, overall administrative costs have been rising 12 to 15 percent per year in most paper-shuffling companies where, incidentally, some studies show up to 90 percent of messages are for internal use only! There is a great need to gain control of and to curtail these startling paper costs.

Office automation can be the force behind an expansion of the data processing department's corporate role into a service able to handle text and data storage, processing, and transmission requirements. There are, of course, significant problems to be faced, and there are retarding forces. The major problem is people. It is felt on three levels:

- On the ground level is the acute shortage of the experienced software engineers who are needed to design and implement distributed office systems.
- On the next level is a staff that must operate the systems in the day-to-day environment.
- On the top level is basic acceptance of these "strange new approaches" by the management of the firm.

The drives behind change are higher productivity, lower cost, and the technology with which those goals can be reached. The favorable economics of substantial investment in new office systems has in recent years been given a big boost by a revolution in semiconductor development. Semiconductors have brought about a virtual explosion of cost-cutting and efficiency-increasing procedures in office facilities and management. A large part of the procedural change has been the implementation of more and more distributed information services.

Opportunities for cost reduction in the storage of information are becoming truly mind-boggling. Since 1960 the price per bit (*binary digit*) of stored information has dropped from 1000 to 1! This is not an across-the-board figure, but if similar developments had occurred in the automobile industry in the same time frame, we'd be purchasing our cars for under $50 and in a couple of years, at the rate new developments are coming, for $5!

The price of stored information will also keep getting lower as new technology develops. For example, the new optical disk being pioneered by Philips (Magnavox), IBM, MCA, Pioneer, Olympus, and Hitachi can store 500,000 pages. About the same size as an LP record, the disk is read by a laser beam, and it will constitute the microfile support of the future.

Imaginative applications seem to be around the corner. In an early program that combines computer controls with video image, General Motors has developed videodisks as sales tools that let customers ask questions about a car and see video answers in response. MIT engineers have created a "moving map" of Aspen, Colorado that lets a viewer plot a route through the ski resort on a map shown on the screen and then see what it would look like to the driver of a car.

With the applications capabilities being enormously expanded, the critical questions in system design should then be: Does the information structure contribute to output and profits? Are the decisions directed toward getting results? Do we give our people the means of providing better service?

Text and data, experience teaches us, should be kept in the form they have been received, that is, the transaction level. In the higher-up layers in the organization, middle management's allocation and optimization decisions and top management's decision support services should be based on the computer power to construct and format the interactive reports needed for the conduct of business. The coming databases will contain qualitative information as well as quantitative data. They will be composed of

- Hard numbers, subject to objective verification
- Softer, future-oriented numbers and comments

The latter will be significant in meeting strategic planning objectives and for reporting on performance from sales to manufacturing and finance. Further attempts will be made to provide better descriptions of uncertainties in both historical and future data and to assure reliable testing of alternatives—the what-if question.

Past-oriented information will be separated into specific classes. A growing demand already exists for the analysis of changes over time and for the presentation of data in a way that assists users in comprehending the pattern of "cost and profit" in the reporting entity. *Forecast disclosure* is a precise example of future data that will become significant in the evaluation of managerial performance. It will apply the same discipline to senior management as that management applies down the line.

In connection with decision support systems, new management practices become possible through computers and communications as data communication and databasing capabilities expand. An example is *differential disclosure*, a technique which will most likely characterize report presentation. Its rationale is that different data is needed by different users of financial or other reports, and disclosure requirements should reflect those differences. One of the most sophisticated aspects will be the construction of operating statements which project a balance between long-term cash inflows and outflows at variable levels of activity and taxation.

Furthermore, productivity and profit-and-loss (P&L) requirements will call for reporting formats available on real enough time (RET) and focusing on the cost and effectiveness of different services, the measurement of outputs, and the relation of each of them to standards. The implementation of such sweeping reporting changes calls for a sharp redefinition of managerial roles and corresponding responsibilities.

Beyond the role of traditional analysis, management's responsibility, productivity, and long-term cost-effectiveness will increasingly be measured and interactively reported. Are the outputs being obtained at minimum costs? What can be done to improve them? What are our alternatives? Which of our options is the best one? What are the long-term effects?

Calendar Services

The new computer-supported services become so much more important to management now that the economic waters are rougher and more swiftly changing than ever before. An enterprise today is faced with the task of tearing down and rebuilding age-old structures while it continues to provide services to its customers. This is a time of trouble and experimentation, of danger and opportunity.

The nature of the business a company is in will help determine which way the company should reorganize its resources so that it can compete profitably. The array of new shapes, designs, and implementations of information systems offers significant opportunities for choice, with productivity improvement the goal. But management must decide which of the available possibilities it wishes to implement through an assessment of the environment and a definition of the most attractive solutions.

The keyword in choosing the proper supporting facilities should be rationality. In most pre-DIS (distributed information system) offices, secretarial and clerical personnel at all levels use expensive time poring over files, transcribing shorthand, hand-editing rough text material, and typing and sending multitudes of letters and reports. Tight-scheduled executives lose valuable time waiting. With computers and communications, instead of waiting, these executives will use video displays tied to microprocessors that control routine office work. Thus, machines will handle such time-consuming tasks as:

- Message and letter input
- Store and forward
- Message and letter delivery
- Interactive communications of all kinds
- Letter typing and telex through electronic mail services
- Facsimile exchange and reproduction through viewdata (transmission of data via an ordinary TV set over telephone lines)

In Chapter 3 we spoke of time management. In time management it is important to recognize the power to minimize, control, and possibly eliminate interruptions—most particularly, that great time-killer the telephone. This is a basic service we ask office automation to perform. The methodology is in the making, as we will see when we talk of interactive videotex and voice mail.

Right now we have the technology to take most of the human labor out of telephoning, interoffice communications, and time-consuming teleprinter and data terminal usage. Many clerical-type functions can be integrated easily by use of the proper computer interfaces. Virtually all of the various steps necessary for the creation of internal or external documents can be automated.

Through store-and-forward functions we can hook many senders on the same line; we can use the technique for delayed delivery of messages to fit a busy executive's schedule and not break his or her concentration and multiplexed voice and data communications. That is the way technology goes—and with it economy.

Typically, each workplace in a DIS network is equipped with stored programs able to handle local requirements. For example, a department manager, at the touch of a few function keys, can look up figures on current expenditures versus budget, daily or hourly output versus production goals, the status of inventory, market penetration of his sales force, client files, credit information, or the personal files of any of his staff.

Generally speaking, the manager of tomorrow will come into the office in the morning, sit down at a personal terminal (most likely a color video unit), and call up an index of what is in the electronic mailbox. He or she can ask for incoming emergencies and flash reports and select any or all of the documents for display on the screen. No more in- and pending-baskets filled with piles of paper.

To check on key commitments and due dates that might be approaching, the manager may invoke the follow-up file, which will list all items in chronological order and be updated as any new items come in. No more cumbersome tickler files. Next to be displayed may be the daily calendar—first the highlights and then the details of appointments or perhaps a look at the rest of the week. The manager may call the phone log to see what messages are awaiting—and do all this work speedily without touching a piece of paper or dealing with another person directly.

Because workstations will be linked, users will be able to channel through and access files at other workstations in the same facility or at remote locations, provided they have the necessary authorization. In that sense, office automation might become the prime vehicle for decision support systems in the late 1980s if we plan the developing services the right way. Such planning calls for the consideration of different viewpoints in evaluating the problems we will be faced with:

1. Technical
2. Commercial
3. Normalization (tariffication, standardization)
4. Applicative
5. Functional

A company wishing to clarify its own thinking on the matter will be well advised to proceed step by step with a comprehensive feasibility study to be followed by a detailed analysis, depending on the results. That is, in fact, the course that has been taken by the International Telephone and Telegraph Consultative Committee (CCITT) which is looking at teletex not as a product, but as a new philosophy in the communications environment. CCITT has set up two commissions to provide the needed recommendations:

- Commission 1 works on machine-to-machine procedures.
- Commission 2 addresses itself to the terminals.

The expected recommendations will cover all aspects of office automation—text preparation, retrieval, and communication—both for the existing networks and for those under development (circuit, packet, and message switching).

"Tomorrow" is already happening today. It demands innovative thinking: new concepts, approaches, policies, attitudes, and practices. As we all know (but tend to forget), the successful implementation of information systems inevitably requires a great deal of preparatory work on the user's behalf. With computers and communications, the time to start such preparatory work is *now*.

Interactive Videotex

The developments we are reviewing have one aim in common: the end user. The user's access to the information services should require no special skills—just the sort of expertise we have known for nearly three decades among systems specialists. Technology can be quite user-friendly. *The computer is not the cold neighbor that the "giant brain" imagery once suggested. Actually, it is the lens of the mind's eye.*

Computers and communications are both the agents and the vehicles of change. And we know by experience that the more diverse technology's components are, the greater the information exchange that has to take place to master them. Also, however, the greater the integration of resources, the greater the benefit—provided the work is done right.

In the new field of computers and communications, videotex (interactive message services) fills both a private and an organizational need. By providing visual communication between man and information, it broadens the horizon of man's mind. Typically, in a public videotex service, there will be a computer and a viewdatabase at the telephone exchange. The end user can reach the pages in the viewdatabase through a TV set with numeric keypad only, a business terminal with alphanumeric keyboard, or an *editing* terminal with multiple functions.

An editing terminal gives organizations that provide information to public and private videotex services a range of facilities for the creation and maintenance of information frames. Editing can usually be done in multiple colors, and it involves alphanumeric characters, graphics, and background. Such a terminal consists of three interconnected elements:

1. A color video display unit (TV) suitable for the alphanumeric characters and graphic symbols
2. An editing control box containing the needed circuitry: a video printer, a cassette tape recorder, and (optional) a built-in modem with a V23 interface (CCITT standard)
3. An extended keyboard for generating the alphanumeric characters and graphic symbols with keys grouped in six separate functional clusters

A graphic cluster (eight keys) is used to compose the graphic symbols by controlling the individual picture elements. Cursor control moves the cursor over the screen. Other control capabilities are provided; examples are copy background page in foreground page, clear foreground page, stop at first character of next word, and wrap around.

The information sent over telephone lines can serve an unlimited number of users. This is a two-way system that lets users select and even modify text and data. The names of videotex services vary from country to country, but "videotex" has now been adopted by the CCITT as generic for all services that display databases on TV sets.

There are two varieties of videotex. One-way broadband communication is *broadcasting videotex*: information can be transmitted via TV signals. Two-way interactive communication using the telephone lines is *interactive videotex*. In either case it presents interesting possibilities for use in business and home information services.

You may ask why, when so many potential user companies already have computers, they should wish to buy videotex as well. The main reason is that videotex is designed to be considerably less expensive than most other computer systems. It is a general-purpose, packaged service with TV-type terminals supporting color that costs nearly an order of magnitude less than the classical computers.

Interactive videotex can serve a purpose in office automation by applying computer power to costly and time-consuming paperwork problems. Most important, videotex can support, in a user-friendly way, the very important fourth layer we have spoken about, that of man-information communication—the end user facility (Figure 33). The nice thing about videotex is that you don't have to know anything about computers—you just have to know your own business.

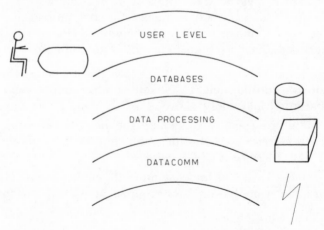

FIGURE 33. Interactive videotex can effectively support the end user facilities.

Interactive videotex capability can be offered to the user—bank, industry, merchandising outlet, or private citizen (who is the ultimate consumer)—through two channels: long-haul and in-house systems. Not only do the two not contradict; they actually support one another through the medium of *communicating viewdatabases.*

Long-haul videotex is provided through a public utility: a telephone company (telco), a value-added network, or a company-operated and -maintained data transmission facility. Messages may travel through voice-grade lines [usually 1200 bits per second (BPS)]. And videotex offers the possibility of two-way communications. The user can both receive and send data through the network *as if* it were a voice communication, but it involves text, data, and image.

Potential for imaginative applications in the broad home information systems category is far-reaching. Home users can communicate directly with the computer storing the information. They can interrogate and get realtime answers. They can not only request further pages but reply to questions, send messages, play games with the computer, or do calculations on taxes and mortgages, projected utility costs, and the like.

It is possible for a home user to make a direct purchase by supplying a credit card number in response to an advertisement. And videotex can also be used to send bank statements to the clients of banks participating in the system. It is a new experience, and as such it has a lot of glamor. It's an experience which will change our way of looking at things, just as the auto has changed our mode of transportation, television, our mode of entertainment, and the airplane, our concept of distances between cities and entire continents.

The private user with a personal computer can attach the machine to the system and then communicate with databases, send and receive electronic mail, and do office work remotely. With all that being already true, it is hard to resist the conclusion that videotex will have a major effect on society in the not-too-distant future. Information exchange creates consciousness and sets the pace of development. Computers handle information; information means knowledge; and *knowledge is power.*

The technical literature has brought into being a new terminology associated with the videotex facilities. A service operator (SO) is a TV broadcasting network or telecommunications common carrier that provides a public service. An organization that serves as the repository for one or more databases on a public videotex service is called an *information provider* (IP).

Typically, a public videotex service will support a closed user group (CUG): a well-defined association (or group) of users who have exclusive rights to certain databases. Whether the videotex service is public or private, its implementation involves organizational prerequisites, transport facilities, warehousing capabilities (data, text), and user-friendly reporting characteristics.

Those of us old enough to have experienced the Paleolithic Age of computing recall the misconceptions which filled the air at that time, even among specialists. Man-machine communication was a tightly guarded secret known only to the privileged few. But as society needs computers to move into higher levels of sophistication, "intelligent machines" become commonplace. In the 100 years of its usage, telephony traveled over a similar curve. *Eventually, only those who can work with computer-based products will be able to find jobs and prosper.*

Acronyms and Abbreviations

AI	artificial intelligence
ANSI	American National Standards Institute
AP	applications programming
ATM	automated teller machine
BSC	binary synchronous communications
BPS	bits per second
BPW	bits per word
CAD/CAM	computer-aided design and manufacture
CCITT	Consultative Committee for International Telephone and Telegraph
CEO	chief executive officer
CGS	Core Graphics System
CO	cutomer organization
CPU	central processing unit
CQL	canonical query language
CUG	closed user group
DB	database, databasing
DBMS	database management system
DC	data communications
DDB	distributed databases
DIS	distributed information system(s)
DOS	disk operating system

DP	data processing
DS	decision support
DSS	decision support system
EFT	electronic funds transfer
Email	electronic mail
Esystem	expert system
EUF	end user functions
4GL	fourth-generation languages
5GL	fifth-generation languages
GKS	Graphics Kernel System
HW	hardware
IE	information element
I/O	input/output
IP	information provider
ISO	International Standards Organization
Isoft	integrated software
KB	keyboard
kbit	kilobits
kBPS	kilobits per second
Kbytes	1024 bytes
LAN	local area networks
LHN	long-haul networks
Mbit	M = mega, or million, bits
MBPS	megabits per second
Mbytes	M = mega, or million, bytes
MIPS	million instructions per second
MIS/DP	management information systems/data processing
Mpixels	M = mega, or million, pixels
ms/byte	microseconds per byte
MTBF	mean time between failures
NBS	National Bureau of Standards
OA	office automation
OS	operating system
OSI	Open System Interconnection model
P&L	profit and loss

PBX	private branch exchange
PC	personal computer
PCB	printed-circuit board
POS	point of sale
RET	real enough time
RT	realtime
SIGGRAPH	Special Interest Group on Computer Graphics of the Association for Computing Machinery
SO	service operator
SW	software
TDB	text and database
VDI	virtual device interface
VLSI	very large scale integration
WP	word processing
WS	workstation

Index

ABOUT THE AUTHOR

Dr. Dimitris Chorafas has been involved in the computer field since 1953 in various capacities, including programmer, analyst, designer, project manager, and for the last 25 years consultant to the presidents of major corporations. His projects have ranged from top-level company reorganization to information systems architecture, computer design, and strategic software decisions. Since 1961 he has been an international corporate consultant. That status, combined with his being a university professor, has taken him to 60 different countries. Over the last 20 years, he has specialized in realtime operations, mini- and microcomputers, the reduction of systems expenditures, and the optimization of DP usage, both equipment and personnel. Dr. Chorafas has written numerous technical articles, is the author of 40 books, and has been published in 16 countries.